Wno Knew?

It's All About You Because Everyone Is A Salesperson!

It's All About You!

RICHARD F. LIBIN

ISBN: 0692789353

ISBN-13: 978-0692789353 (Automotive Profit Builders, Inc.)

Automotive Profit Builders, Inc.

P.O. Box 2011

Natick, MA 01760

Tel: (508) 626-9200

Email: rlibin@apb.cc

www.richardlibin.com

www.who-knew.com

First edition published 2017.

Editor: Bonnie Quintanilla

Production: Corridor Communications, Inc.

People Are Talking About Who Knew?

"This book hits the nail on the head. In Who Knew? Richard Libin presents the kind of acquired skills a person needs to be a successful sales professional. He understands that the sale has more to do with the person than with the product or service itself."

—Jeff Gonsalves, Law Enforcement Professional

"Great content! Great format! Like Mr. Libin's first book, Who Stopped the Sale?, Who Knew? provides essential information and reminders for sales professionals from a pro who knows. This book will help you make customers happier and sell more at the same time."

—Steve Finlay, Writer, Automotive Industry

"In Who Knew?, Richard Libin again has written an industry standard. If you want to profit in sales, this is the book you need to succeed."

—Deanna Juarez, CEO, Evolve Fitness

"Richard Libin has guided thousands to success and, with Who Knew?, he shows us all how to maximize our potential. An easy read that packs punch, Who Knew? provides essential fundamentals and timeless advice on how to work more effectively with people every day. All books should be this valuable and direct at making their points. I recommend this book to anyone who leads, manages, works, coaches or parents—after all, we're all salespeople, like it or not!!"

—Jenn Smith, Law Enforcement Professional

"I'm from the school of thought that if you're going to put the time and energy into learning, then learn from the best. Richard Libin is a master at his craft and in Who Knew? his knowledge is conveyed in a style that makes a quick and easy read. Once I began to read the book, I couldn't put it down. Richard Libin gets my thumbs up whole-heartedly.

—Paul Tortora, Retired Superintendent of Schools, Trawler Specialist, Connecticut

Dedication

I know you never thought I listened to you, but not a day goes by when I don't think about or use something you taught me. Who knew? This one's for you, Mom.

This book would not have been possible without the love and support of my family, my wife Cathy, my daughter Jennifer and my son Michael. I am so proud of you all and appreciate the confidence and love you've given me. You continue to inspire and teach me every single day.

"Choose to be positive."

Contents

It's All About You!

Preface

WHO KNEW? THIS book is about you!

It doesn't matter what you do, where you come from or where you're headed. This book is for you. Why? Because everyone is a salesperson. Mothers sell new foods to children. Individuals sell their experience and expertise to land new jobs. Customers sell banks or utility companies on reasons they should waive annoying fees. Employees sell their performance to win promotions and raises. Politicians sell promises to get elected. The list goes on. Every day from the time you get up in the morning until the time you go to bed at night you negotiate, communicate and influence the way people think to sell something.

Virtually anyone who is successful in any endeavor is constantly selling someone something, whether or not they work as a salesperson. Selling is an essential skill and like it or not, we all have to sell to succeed. The American author, Robert Louis Stevenson, recognized this when he said, "Everyone lives by selling something." Selling is part of our way of life. Most of the time you don't even realize that you are selling, but you are.

According to the United States Bureau of Labor Statistics, one in nine, almost 36 million Americans work in sales. They persuade people to purchase products and services ranging from homes and telephones to insurance, cars and more. Over the years, however, through poor behavior and techniques, bad experiences and portrayals by the media in films such as *Death of a Salesman* and *Glen Gary Glen Ross*, salespeople have earned a negative perception. Many of the best business schools and universities avoid teaching courses on how to sell, and students and other individuals avoid learning good sales techniques. As a result, many who embrace sales as a career are not properly trained or qualified, and don't truly understand how to sell. In the end, buyers continue to have poor experiences and the negative stereotypes are perpetuated.

You have the ability to change this. Who knew?

Most people believe that selling means persuading someone to purchase a product or service. This is where salespeople and sales in general start to fail. Effective selling starts with the customer, not with what you are trying to sell. A salesperson's job – regardless of what they are selling – is to help customers select the right product or service, the one that fits their needs, wants and desires. It doesn't matter what industry you work in; it's a buyer's market. Customers have the power. If they don't like the experience they are getting, they can easily leave and go to a competitor. So, what kind of experience do you want to give them?

Learning to sell more effectively will bring substantial rewards and opportunities, whether in everyday life or as a professional salesperson. Since we all are born salespeople and we all sell every day, why not choose to be the best salesperson you can be?

"Create change."

SECTION 1

Are You A Creature of Habit?

It's All About You!

*Innovation creates
positive improvements.*

It's All About You!

Introduction

A CREATURE OF habit is defined as a person who "develops (generally inadvertently) a set pattern of doing the same thing(s) during a certain time period of the day, week, etc."

In some ways, we are all creatures of habit. Everyone has a routine that they follow. What we don't realize is that this routine traps us into thinking and working inside the proverbial box and acting in our comfort zone in our personal and professional lives. We drive the same route to work, park in the same space every day, drink the same coffee, shop at the same grocery store and buy the same brands.

I drove from Boston to Canada and then to Baltimore on business trip and relied on my trusty GPS to find and follow the best route like I always do. It took me to a secondary road and then to the highway. About 20 miles down the highway,

I passed a truck. I noticed that it was the exact same truck that I had passed just before leaving the "slower" secondary road to take the highway. The truck driver had taken a different route, a better route, which cut time and mileage off his trip. As a creature of habit, I chose to rely on my GPS, which clearly was not the best choice. If I had known, I could have followed the truck. I learned that checking for alternative routes and times is probably a good idea.

This was a good example of confusing guidance with direction, something many of us do every day. So what's the difference? Guidance is defined as giving advice or counsel. With guidance, you have a choice. When someone gives direction, on the other hand, they instruct a person or group to act or do something in a specific way; they command or order them. With direction, you are expected to do what you are told.

People are creatures of habit. They do things the same way over and over again in same way they have always done it. They don't think about changing, even though there may be a better way to do things. They behave this way in spite of the guidance and alternatives that they get throughout their lives. When they were in school, teachers provided information to guide and influence choices. A GPS system provides guidance—choices—that shows how to move from point to point. At work, managers provide education, training and guidance designed to help their employees excel. While it should be regarded as important, information provided by others, whether from teachers, technology or managers, may not always be the best advice in every situation.

As professionals, our challenge is to realize that people are creatures of habit and then to find ways to help them break those habits. We need to help them get out of their box or comfort zone. We need to help them decide to work with us, to buy from the business we represent and to purchase the product or service we are selling.

The only way to do this is to help people change their thinking. We need to give them a new perspective and, as the saying goes, get them to think and act outside the box. Much of the challenge with this has to do with perception. Two people who look at the exact same picture will each see it differently. One may see the sun breaking through a storm and another may see a storm brewing. Neither perception is wrong. They simply are different. They are formed based on habits and attitudes each person has developed for years, and because of that, it would be rare to see either of these people change their perception.

As creatures of habit, we follow the same routine every day. We drive the same roads, shop at the same stores, eat at the same restaurants, watch the same televisions shows and loyally buy the same make or brand whenever the opportunity arises. How many times have you left for work early just to beat someone else to "your" parking spot? Or, how often do you hear people refer to a television sitcom as "my show?" We live, work and play in the same box, even if the box is not the best we could have chosen.

On the trip described previously, I could have arrived at my destination earlier if I had stepped outside my comfort zone, thought outside the box and considered alternative routes. Instead, I followed the "guidance" provided by my GPS as if there were no other choice. There is always a choice.

Amazing, inspiring and almost unbelievable things can happen when individuals and companies think and work outside the box.

- **Henry Ford** failed and went broke five times before he finally succeeded. In the early days, Ford built cars one at a time. The car sat on the ground as mechanics and their support teams sourced parts and returned to the car to assemble it from the chassis upwards. Henry Ford wanted to "put the world on wheels" and produce an affordable vehicle for the general public. He knew that to do this, he had to produce the largest number of cars with the simplest design for the lowest possible cost, using what he called "a moving assembly line." Ford invented machines, and then kept experimenting until every practice was refined, and his mass production vision became a reality. A bare chassis moved along the line and through different workstations until a complete car was driven off under its own power. Ford's moving assembly line started an industrial revolution. If he had given up, millions may not have had jobs or benefitted from the innumerable products that are now readily accessible and affordable.

- **Dr. Seuss'** first children's book, *And to Think That I Saw It on Mulberry Street*, was rejected by 27 publishers. The 28th publisher, Vanguard Press, sold six million copies of the book. He went on to earn two Academy Awards, two Emmy Awards, a Peabody Award and the Pulitzer Prize, among many others. In fact, one in four children receives Dr. Seuss as their first book. Seuss' birthday, March 2, has been named National Read Across America Day and "Dr Seuss Quotes" gets searched on Google over 135,000 times per month. Can you imagine a world without Dr. Seuss, a man that essentially was told by 27 reviewers to give up?

• **Lee Iacocca**, in what was perhaps his greatest success, looked at a plain Ford Falcon chassis and imagined it with a racy body, a long hood and a short rear deck. Despite having to fight management every step of the way to make his vision a reality, Iacocca prevailed, and created not only the iconic Ford Mustang, but a class of vehicles known as pony cars. The Mustang set a record for first-year sales and has remained in Ford's car lineup as a core vehicle ever since. Later, in the 1980's, his tough management decisions and innovative ideas – all of which he had to fight for – literally saved Chrysler from bankruptcy. While not every car Iacocca conceived was a success, he never stopped inventing. In fact, Ford has re-introduced a new version of the Shelby GT, designed specifically for international sales. Imagine it. A man whose vision no one shared designed and built what are now everlasting American icons.

- **Fred Smith** wrote a term paper based on an idea for reliable overnight delivery service. His professor gave him a "C" because the idea wasn't feasible. Years later, many potential investors agreed with the professor, refusing to send capital Smith's way. The funds he did raise in 1971 and 1972 were gone by 1974, along with his investors. One catchy slogan ("FedEx–when it absolutely, positively has to be there overnight.") and several million dollars of hard-won capital later, Federal Express was on its way to profitability and long-term success. He was called unrealistic; he ran out of money; and people didn't believe in him or his ideas. Because of his willingness to work outside the box, FedEx ships more than 9,000,000 packages each day!

- **Steve Jobs** wanted to give everyone a computer at a time when nobody realized computers were necessary. He founded Apple to create home computers, experienced some early success and even changed advertising with the infamous "1984" commercial that changed the way people thought about computing. Apple faltered in the consumer market with the expensive Macintosh and Jobs was fired from the company he founded, but he was eventually asked to return to his first love, where he restored Apple as a profitable company and innovation leader. Steve Jobs, fired by his board of directors, came back to re-build a company that literally permeates our lives. In the United States, 3.5 million pre-college students use iPads in school; 61% of teens prefer Apple mobile devices; 70% of college freshmen enter school with an Apple computer; and nearly 60% of households own one Apple product with 60% of owning at least two.

- **Walt Disney** was fired by a newspaper editor because "he lacked imagination and had no good ideas." Disney declared bankruptcy several times before he built Disneyland, which was originally rejected by the City of Anaheim. He transformed common household vermin into two of the most beloved, animated characters in the world – Mickey and Minnie Mouse. Sixty years later, people around the world are celebrated something that was built by a guy with no imagination. Who else could ever have thought that two mice would be so famous?

Each and every one of our lives would be dramatically different if these individuals had not seen and done things outside the box. Imagine if they had quit when they were told they had no vision, imagination, ability, concept of reality or ideas. "No" was not part of their vocabulary. They couldn't begin to understand the concept. They had ideas that they believed in. They had faith in their abilities. They didn't care when people told them "no." They pushed on regardless of how hard and challenging it was and despite the many roadblocks they encountered. When one thing didn't work, they moved outside their comfort zones and tried something else. They believed in the adage, "If you are sick of starting over, stop giving up."

Who influenced you the most in your life in terms of teaching you, showing you something new or inspiring you to persevere, to do things differently? In every business, there is always one person that everyone wants to learn from and emulate. It's the person you would follow to a new job just to have the opportunity to keep learning from them. Everyone is influenced by someone. For me, it was Buzzer Mason. He'd call me Kiddo and, among other things, always said, "Just remember, there is an ass for every seat," and "Never give up." Everything he said made so much sense. He had a huge influence on my life and my work. He taught me that it doesn't matter what product you are selling, you have to show it with passion, and if you don't, no one else will ever get excited about it. He taught me how to think differently and to look for new ways of doing things.

None of these individuals – Henry Ford, Dr. Seuss, Lee Iacocca, Fred Smith, Walt Disney, Steve Jobs or Buzzer Mason – are any different from you. They just looked for new ways to do things and then made them happen. Stop for a moment and think. If there is one thing about your job, one responsibility that you absolutely dislike, what is it? Now, think about how you can change or improve it. Think about how you can do it differently so that it becomes more effective and enjoyable. Take responsibility for how and why you dislike that one thing. Proactively work to change it instead of simply blaming the process, system or task and then doing it again the same way you always have.

Think about your professional skills with the same perspective. Find the one thing that you (or others) see as a shortcoming in how you do your job. Ask yourself, "What kind of performer am I? Am I above average, average or below average? What kind do I want to be?" Take responsibility for where you are today and proactively work to change and improve it. Look at yourself, your performance and your skills from a new perspective and discover ways to improve. Start by moving up one notch, and then another and another. Proactively work to make your vision a reality. Then, do it all over again.

Innovation. Continuous improvement. Reinvention. While these words can be powerful and daunting at the same time, each can be realized by thinking out of the box. Change your perspective and proactively pursue a different approach. Change, while scary and even difficult, can bring countless benefits, personally and professionally.

Comfort Zone	Different Way	Personal Benefit	Business Benefit
Vacuum cleaner	iRobot Roomba	Eliminates work	New revenue stream
Checkout line	Self checkout	Faster, easier	Reduced expenses

Comfort Zone	Different Way	Personal Benefit	Business Benefit
Specialty stores (grocery, bakery, hardware, etc.)	Warehouse stores	Convenient, lower prices	Increased revenue; lowered overhead
Bulk packaged foods	Individual servings	Convenient	Increased revenue per product
Electric ovens for all baking and cooking	Microwaves or convection ovens	Convenient, fast, more even cooking	New revenue stream
External hard drives for backup storage	Cloud computing	Increased security and accessibility	Recurring revenue stream

Change, reinvention and finding new ways to do old things, happens every day. Just look at these recent "inventions" that came about simply because someone didn't like the way things had always been done. All it took was one person who decided to think out of the box, to find a different way. Now, we're all benefitting from their determination to change.

The difference between people who stay in their comfort zone and those who think out of the box is a willingness to take risks and a sense of urgency to drive change. And, if the risk doesn't work, their sense of urgency and belief in their vision help them persist, try again and make it work. They never quit. Each of the individuals we looked at, regardless of their field or endeavor, was a risk taker. They left their comfort zone repeatedly. They accomplished exactly what they envisioned and what they often were told would never be possible.

In business, the question you must constantly ask is, "What am I going to do differently tomorrow that I didn't do today?" Success comes when **YOU** think out of the box. Ask yourself:

- How do I communicate?
- How do I communicate with my peers and coworkers?
- Am I always learning about my life and business?
- Am I looking for new things that are coming out?
- Am I willing to learn from everyday experiences?
- Do I look for new ways to solve problems, or am I complacent?

It's easy to stay in your comfort zone, even though we all have the ability to get out of it, if we make a conscious effort to do so. Research shows that most people either procrastinate or approach tasks with a sense of urgency, and that all of us fall into one of these categories when it comes to thinking and acting outside the box.

- **Proactive** – People who take action. Risk takers who take bold steps. Action oriented, innovative individuals.
- **Reactive** – Procrastinators who take action only when forced. These people go to the doctor only when nothing else works.

- **Responsive** – Followers. Easily influenced individuals who go with the flow.

- **Procrastinate** – Followers who are easily distracted and put off tasks until the last minute. They prefer to do it the way someone else has done it.

- **Sense of Urgency** – Leaders who take the initiative and are deadline driven with "can do" positive attitudes. Achievers.

In all honesty, where do you fall? What can you do to become more proactive? Or, if you believe you are proactive, have you done everything possible to become your best? Education, training, books and seminars can offer guidance and make you think, but only you can take yourself out of your comfort zone. Only you can think and act outside the box. Only you can act with a sense of urgency. One thing is certain: if you don't work for change, nothing will change.

It's All About You!

CHAPTER 1

What Does the Brand Stand For?

AT THE HEART of life or business, our desire is to influence others in our favor. This starts at an early age. Babies cry when they need something. Men and women dress for success and to attract others. Politicians campaign to gain votes. Brands advertise to influence buying behavior. Each of these actions is a means of providing information, which others can use to make a decision.

Consumers are hammered by tens of thousands of marketing messages every day. The use of big data and social media analytics helps advertisers specifically tailor each ad directly to a consumer's specific interests. Every day, consumers are unknowingly directed to products and services they may or may not need. Internet searches become ads on email and social media. Sometimes this approach is successful, but rarely does it build loyal clientele or brand loyalists. So, what really makes a difference when it comes to influencing buying decisions?

Every morning, there are people who stop in at their local coffee shop around the same time. When they enter, a server, Judy, for example, smiles and greets them by name and asks if they want the usual. She also suggests a food item, either something new or something they've had before. The store is spotless, music is inviting and not overpowering, there is free Wi-Fi and many of the customers' faces are familiar. When the order is ready, Judy gives them a perfectly crafted, warm beverage. So, why do they stop at this coffee shop and spend so much for coffee every day when there are coffee shops on virtually every corner? Why, despite the fact that they've met friends at one of the others, they keep coming to *this* coffee shop. It's not the coffee, the price or the amenities. It's the relationship. Without fail, the same person gets their coffee every time. They have a relationship. Even when they use the drive-through window, they hear a manager's voice on the speaker. Because they have a relationship and know that the manager and server know them, they can easily banter, like in this conversation.

The customer at the drive-through said, "How come my coffee's not made?" The manager responded, "By the time you get up here, it will be." When the customer arrived at the window, the manager joked, "Can I take your order?" The customer replied, "You mean I have to give you my order?!" The manager said, "Yep, that will be one large coffee with extra cream and extra sugar." He then handed the customer their usual, large black coffee. The customer's relationship was not with the store alone. It was with the people in the store. He knew that whomever started to help him on any particular day, would serve him from start to finish.

When you remove all the brand elements, all you have left are the relationships, the ones with Judy, the manager, and each of the other employees. Their sincere interest, recognition and care make them credible. Judy and her colleagues know that if they want customers to buy, they must build relationships with them. In essence, the people working in this coffee shop have become the brand. People go to this little coffee shop because they know they will be treated like a friend. Like politicians, babies, individuals and brands, the employees at this coffee shop are seeking to influence behavior. The difference is that they have earned credibility. Without credibility, no amount of campaigning or advertising will ever wield any influence.

Credibility and personal service go hand in hand. When people provide personal service they are building a relationship. It is like the catch-phrase on the television show, *Cheers*. Where everybody knows your name. People will be loyal if they have relationships.

The same is true for everyone.

Every person wants to sell more, make more money and perhaps even contribute to higher profits. To do this, people work diligently to influence others in a manner that is favorable to the outcome they desire—a sale. That is one reason there are so many articles in publications from *Entrepreneur Magazine* to *Business Week*, answering the question, "How can I get a customer to buy from me?" These articles usually include a list of reasons, all of which comprise various elements of a brand, including the use of technology, along with marketing, quality, product and price.

Were these the reasons a customer purchased from you this morning, or the caller placed a phone order or a new client hired you? What do you think made the difference? Was it skill? Quality? Responsiveness? Or was it product? Price? Features?

> ## *Your relationship is built on trust.*

First and foremost, it was YOU. Who knew?

It was the credibility you earned by listening, caring, sharing knowledge and guiding the customer to a choice that met each need, want and desire in a product or service. It's this credibility that caused the customer to trust you and that essentially made you synonymous with the brand. Building credibility can lead to sales, profits and commissions, but it must be earned before any of these can happen.

Customers buy brands from people they trust. They need to see, feel and know that the people they are working with can deliver on their words and promises. When salespeople start to think and act like brand ambassadors, they focus on creating positive customer experiences, helping customers find the right product or service for their needs, wants and desires, and building brand loyalty. They are no longer selling; they are helping customers buy. In turn, customers regard brand ambassadors as individuals they can trust and call on whenever they have a need or challenge. Everyone should aspire to be that type of person.

Over several years, I have purchased five cars, two of them from the same dealership, but none of them from the same individual. Why? We had no relationship. They had a lovely, state-of-the-art building, and they had a product that I liked, yet no one represented the brand credibly or proudly. Not once did I hear from any individual after I made my purchase. The impression I had was that they took the money and moved on without any concern for me or my business.

Customers must have trust and confidence in the people they are working with, not just the product or service. When trust is earned, it is extended to the brand represented. Only then can anyone begin to influence behavior and sales.

What is credibility? It is a perceived value and a trust that customers have as a result of interacting and relating. Credibility can only be earned by gaining the trust and confidence of others. It comes when customers see certain factors or qualities applied consistently. Once credibility is established, a customer becomes very comfortable doing business with an individual and rarely hesitates to contact that one person for anything. A relationship has been formed.

What helps forge this connection? It is commitment and dedication. For example, I went to visit a potential customer in Kansas simply because the decision maker wanted to meet me. He had a contract in hand for more than six months, but would not make a decision. I spent $700 on a plane ticket, $100 on a hotel and $200 for transportation, $1,000 in all for one night. He signed the contract and asked me to return to personally manage the installation because we developed a relationship.

Earning credibility requires a conscious and consistent effort. It can't be given or assumed; it must be earned with customers. Credibility is a form of feedback that you get from others. It is a reflection of who you are, what you do and what you represent. It is the greatest compliment you could ask for in business.

There are innumerable ways to earn credibility, all of which must come from a genuine intent. For example, credibility may be earned by:

- Placing a well-being call, a simple call to be sure everything is okay, to ask how the customer is doing. This call enables you to face any challenges or problems head on rather than letting them fester.

- Driving an hour and 15 minutes or getting on a plane to see a customer.

- Listening to a customer's challenges and making referrals that may help.

- Shaking hands, promising to return and doing so.

- Sending a handwritten note or email personally, or calling to check in again after a visit.
- Getting together for lunch or a cup of coffee.
- Communicating like a human being, showing your personality and actively participating in the conversation by talking about your interests, your family, your hobbies and so on.

Still not convinced? Perhaps this unsolicited testimonial will do the trick.

There is a not-so-local equipment and apparatus company we use sometimes. The same person calls on us regularly, even when we're not anticipating any purchases. Often, he just stops by to tell us something noteworthy within our local fire department region or to leave us with a newsletter about some new training procedure or new product we have not seen before. The folks at the fire station love him because he seems to be all about making sure we look at him as a resource or for product recommendations. It seems he is always asking questions. I was even greeted the other day with, "Hey, Rod. I know you folks are saving up for a new personal protective equipment extractor. You may want to look at the one I just sold to your mutual-aid department to the west. The chief will be happy to walk you through it anytime you want to go over it." Somehow, I'm not sure how, he just knew what our plans were. He leaves us his company's catalog and makes it very easy to place orders. And although I know very little about the actual company he works for, he provides us with value every time we come in contact with him. So, you might say that the salesperson and his relationship with us are the most important factors in our purchasing decision. To us, he is the company.

It's All About You!

CHAPTER 2

Helping Customers Get the Best Experience Possible

THE LATE AMERICAN entrepreneur, author and personal development speaker Jim Rohn said, "One customer, well taken care of, could be more valuable than $10,000 worth of advertising." It's true. Giving customers the best possible experience is the surest way to create a customer experience that builds loyalty, sales and profits. Whether walking into a store, talking to an individual on the phone or meeting in an office, customers should feel like they are welcome and belong. There is one person who is responsible for ensuring that welcoming quality is reflected in every point of interaction: YOU. Who knew?

When my son was 12, he took a lawnmower, went around the neighborhood and started mowing lawns for pay. Pretty soon he was mulching and then planting gardens. In college, he rented a garage for his equipment and today, he owns a successful landscaping construction business that grows year after year. The best business advice I ever gave him was, "It doesn't make any difference what you charge someone to do a job. What matters is your word. If you tell a client what you plan to do, when it will be done and the cost, you better deliver. If you can't be there, call a week ahead and tell them when you will be there. People want your word to matter. When it does, they don't care about price." To this day, the only reason he loses a job is because he can't get to it quick enough because he has so much business.

At my company, Automotive Profit Builders (APB), we consider this the Red Carpet Treatment. We believe that every person who walks through the door must receive it. The Red Carpet Treatment is, in essence, the simplest definition of customer service, the act of serving the customer, of creating the best possible customer experience and helping the customer get what they need, want and desire. It is an approach that sets the Four Seasons Resorts apart from other large hotels, for example.

At the Four Seasons, guests are met by a greeter and welcomed (often by name). Another greeter then takes their bags without being asked, while another opens the door and guides them to the check-in. The person with the bags waits while the guests check. They are given the room information and seemingly disappear, only to be waiting at the room with the bags when the guests arrive. The attendant introduces himself and places the bags where the guests wants them, shows the guests around the room, gets the ice and asks if anything else is needed before leaving. No matter which Four Seasons you visit, this arrival treatment is consistently the same. Most hotels strive to deliver this caliber of service. Yet as many hotel brands become larger their service wanes. For example, this arrival experience, which we've all experienced. You arrive at the hotel and a valet asks if you are checking in and whether or not you need help with your bags. The staff unloads the bags and takes them through another entrance leaving you to find registration desk and go to your room. After a time, the bellboy eventually arrives at your room, unloads your bags and stands, waiting for a tip. Which experience delights the customer?

It's the same for any business. When you take care of customers, they will buy and become loyal clients. Know the game plan, make it happen and delight the customer in the process. This is the core responsibility of everyone working in any business and it should be done simply and purely because it is part of doing the best job possible.

All too often, in the effort to provide the Red Carpet Treatment, people focus on what shouldn't happen (negative) during a customer experience instead of what should happen (positive). As a result, the negative becomes a self-fulfilling prophecy. For example, consider the person who has a job interview after lunch who thinks repeatedly, "I can't spill, I can't spill, I can't spill, I can't spill…" Splat, there goes the dressing, right on his shirt or tie. Focusing on the negative makes it a reality. Where you focus can mean the difference between a good day and a bad day. We've all had one of *THOSE* days: you wake up late, the coffee maker doesn't start and you hit traffic because of an accident ahead. In your mind, you think, "Great. This is going to be one of *THOSE* days." All day long this streak continues, and as you go to sleep you think, "I KNEW it would be a bad day." At the end of the day, you went home and hadn't disappointed yourself. You had the kind of day you wanted to have.

What if instead, you thought, "Wow, I'm lucky I woke up late and the coffee maker didn't start. I might have been in that accident, if I'd been on time. It's going to be a great day!" It is like the story of *The Little Engine That Could* who kept saying, "I think I can, I think I can, I think I can…" until he could finally say, "I thought I could, I thought I could, I thought I could!"

Your Choice

Where you focus – on the negative or on the positive – shapes the outcome of every action you take. People who focus on not losing sales will lose more sales because they are focusing on a negative outcome. They won't disappoint themselves and in the end they can say, "We told you so." The people who focus on increasing sales adopt a positive attitude and every bit of their energy goes into making the focus a reality. At the end of the day, they won't be disappointed either, but they will say, "We knew it would be a good day!" People who believe they can will proactively find a way to put together a deal.

It is human nature to say or focus on what we don't want to happen when asked, without ever realizing it. As such, we need to make a conscious effort to focus on what we want to happen in order to achieve positive outcomes. Start by making and keeping these three commitments:

1. Focus on what you want and say it to yourself out loud and in your mind repeatedly throughout each day: "I will _____."

2. Monitor yourself so that you are aware of your focus and can be proactive in redirecting it toward the positive. A positive focus gets positive results.

3. Practice. Be persistent. Write down what you want and picture it in your head. Never disappoint yourself. Be proud of what you can achieve when you focus on the positive.

You have a choice. The glass is either half empty or half full. What will your focus be? By focusing on the positive, on what you want to do for and give to the customer, you will be taking the first steps toward delivering the Red Carpet Treatment.

There is a printing business in Southern California that provides the Red Carpet Treatment before customers ever leave their cars. Every parking spot in their lot has a sign in front of it with a unique saying, like these:

- Reserved for our VIP Customer – That's everyone including YOU!
- Reserved for our Customer of the Day – That's everyone including YOU!

The signs and message are the icing on the cake and designed to make the customer feel good. The real benefit is that the company gives the customers what they want – convenient, reserved parking.

An article in the *Daily Finance* provided different anecdotes of exemplary Red Carpet Treatment, which are clear examples of the people who focused on what they wanted: closing a sale and pleasing the customer.

"I was looking for a certain apron and there were not any on the sales floor. A person in the housewares department asked me to leave my cell phone number and said that she would personally go into the backroom to look through the boxes and call me when she had finished. About four hours later, my cell phone rang and sure enough it was the

individual telling me she had found a box of the aprons and would be happy to ring it up over the phone and send it to package pickup for me. Wow, what a great employee."

In another story, a lady was looking for a book for her son for Christmas and had asked the service desk in her local bookstore to help.

"The person working looked in the computer to see if they had the book. The computer showed that some were arriving in the next few days; however, they would not be in time. The employee found the book at another store and told the customer that she could have the book in thirty minutes. The employee went out, bought the book and had it for the customer when she returned from her other shopping."

That's the Red Carpet Treatment. The employee went above and beyond to help the customer and to make sure she still did business with the store rather than sending her somewhere else.

Every consumer is looking for three things:

1. a product they can buy,

2. a place they can do business with and

3. a person with whom they feel comfortable working.

That's why it is so important that every customer receives consistent treatment. Consistently providing the Red Carpet

Treatment reassures customers that this is their preferred business and reaffirms their decision not to go elsewhere.

In Hollywood, we all know the Red Carpet literally means to roll out a red carpet. But what does this mean in business? When people go out of their way to make sure customers get a warm feeling about the individuals they deal with and the business with which they are working, they are rolling out the Red Carpet Treatment. While having a positive focus or attitude is essential, training on how to deliver the Red Carpet Treatment is equally or even more important. If people aren't trained and don't know what the Red Carpet Treatment means in their business, then all too often, customers end up with the "luck of the draw."

Webster's defines luck of the draw as, "the results of chance, the lack of any choice or sarcasm meaning the person was actually unlucky." No customer anywhere should ever feel like they worked with an individual because of "the luck of the draw." Every customer, regardless of who they are, what they look like, what they are shopping for, how they are dressed or any other factor, should always be treated with the same Red Carpet Treatment. Businesses forget that the customer always has the power in the relationship. Customers who feel like they got the "luck of the draw"—whether because of a negative attitude or lack of training—have a choice. They can simply leave, go to another business or shop online. If they choose to stay, they may become demanding, unreasonable and even agitated.

Customers come in with a game plan. They want to find the best solution, have the best experience at the best value and make their purchase where they feel comfortable. It all starts with customer expectations. For example, the 10-foot rule states that people who are within 10 feet of any and all customers should go out of their way to interact, even if it's just a greeting. The corollary states that if people are within 20 feet of customers, they move into their 10-foot radius and then practice the 10-foot rule. Think about mâitre-d's at a restaurant who always finds their way to a table, just after the main course is served. They typically ask the same questions, "How is everything? Can I get you anything else?" They make a point to find customers and specifically ask what they can do for them. They don't rely on information from the waitstaff. They get it firsthand because they are there to serve you, the customer.

Unfortunately, time and time again, customers leave stores feeling like they just had the worst luck of the draw imaginable. It would be like going to see your personal physician, being put in a room and in walks a doctor you've never seen. How would that make you feel? Customers have a choice. There is always someone else ready to take their money.

The *Daily Finance* also provided examples where the Red Carpet Treatment was lacking.

Story 1: *"Last year, I went to Books-A-Million to buy a children's book for a grandchild. I went to the customer service counter in the center of the store and provided the title and asked where to find it. The person waved her arm in the direction of the children's book section and said, 'Over there.' As I walked away, I heard her turn to her co-worker and say in an aggravated tone, 'She didn't even TRY to find it on her own.'"*

Is this the kind of treatment you want? Is this the kind of place where you want do to business? This is not Red Carpet Treatment. Does this treatment build relationships? Does it make customers want to spend their money with this business? Consider what might have happened instead if the person looked up the title, found it was in stock and walked the customer to the shelf to find the book? What would have happened then? The customer stopped at the counter because she wanted help finding the book without wasting time, where the person could provide exact directions. This customer was not browsing. She was there to buy. If I were that customer, I would have turned around, asked the person if she had something to say and then would have thought carefully about whether or not I wanted to do business with that particular store.

Story 2: *"I recently drove into the auto wing of a major retailer and stood at the counter to check in. The person* *behind the counter was dealing with another customer. Ten to 15 minutes later, she was still dealing with the customer, and while doing so stated to another colleague that she was finished working in 20 minutes. She was going between the back and front of the office, typing on her computer and not once did she even look at me. I asked two other people working there if there was someone who could help me. They just pointed to her. Needless to say, I just got in my car and drove out."*

In this case, if the person had focused on the positive choices she could have given the customer what she wanted. First, she should have acknowledged the customer, told her that someone would be with her in a few minutes and asked if she minded waiting. The person then should have immediately asked a colleague to help. If the delay was going to be significant, she should have updated the customer or perhaps given her paperwork to fill out while waiting. Here, the customer simply wanted to be acknowledged.

Focusing on the positive, learning how your business delivers the Red Carpet Treatment and training or practicing in its delivery, will create the kind of customer experience needed so that no customer ever gets the luck of the draw.

Building a powerful brand is important to the success of any business. However, consistently delivering on your customer promise every single day and in every customer interaction is what makes a powerful, sustainable business.

Physical, communication, human and sensory interactions between a business and a client all can create unforgettable experiences. For many businesses, the most powerful place where businesses touch their customers is in stores. However, market leaders understand that every minute interaction, from a phone call or email or inquiry to a "why buy here" brochure, is a point of interaction that can affect the customer experience and influence perception.

Points of interaction are the means in which brands deliver on their promise, where they can thrive and develop loyal clientele or fail miserably. We live, work and play in a networked environment where the Internet, instant messaging, blogging and mobile devices make word-of-mouth reviews instantly viral. Positive and negative points of interaction grow exponentially and can become the tipping point that can have far-reaching consequences. That's why it is crucial to deliver a consistent customer experience at every detail.

Consistency separates the most admired customer-centric companies from the rest. For example, you always know exactly what you are going to get from Apple. In fact, the employees are required to put on their Apple shirts at the store, so that they are not bombarded with questions outside the store and that the company can be paid for its expertise and information. Disney has cast members that provide exceptional experiences, yet you never see them in their uniforms outside the parks, a rule that helps protect their brand. Finally, Southwest Airlines prides itself on offering the best experience for the lowest price in the air. They have an exceptionally positive, "no problem" attitude—within their corporate boundaries—from being overly friendly and comical, to serving drinks or peanuts. You always know what you get when you fly Southwest. These brands excel because they strive for consistency and their people deliver on the brand promise. These companies have defined and consistently radiate their identity at each and every point of interaction. Consistency across every point of interaction is by far the hardest part of delivering an exceptional customer experience. As such, it is a powerful differentiator.

Without a doubt, every single consumer in North America and beyond has experienced inconsistency in the customer experience. This real-life example demonstrates how inconsistencies can negatively impact or minimally, neutralize the customer experience.

Before one business trip, I called a Marriott hotel directly to book a room because, in my experience, going directly to the hotel provided me with more options and better service than trying to book through another avenue. After reaching someone, I asked about any special offers or discounts but was told that none were available, so I booked the room at the full rate. On arrival, I presented my card. The person at the registration desk asked why I hadn't booked at a preferred rate. Without waiting for a reply, my reservation was upgraded, my cost dropped and I was given a list of amenities that I could enjoy at no charge, including in-room Wi-Fi, breakfast and local calls. When I checked out, I was presented with a bill that did not reflect any of these complimentary amenities. I pointed out the discrepancy, and the person working that day took my bill with a heavy sigh, made changes, reprinted it and placed it on the counter, all without a word but with a look that could have shot daggers. I worked with three people and had three very different experiences. There could be a hundred reasons for the inconsistency and attitude of each of these individuals, from having a bad day or a lack of training to feeling sick to simply not caring.

From the customer's perspective, however, none of those reasons matter; their "Marriott" experience was akin to riding a roller coaster. It started off bumpy and then rose to a high at check-in, only to end on a rickety note that left me feeling like I had imposed on the clerk when I asked for the adjustments. The worst part was that my impression of this particular Marriott hotel was negative, despite the fact that the location was convenient, the amenities were good and the room was pleasant and quiet. From the hotel's perspective, there were at least three (if not more) distinct processes where the people, procedures or technology interfered with the overall customer experience. The three processes were reservation, check-in and checkout. While I may hesitate to stay at this location, my overall impression of Marriott remains high because I have had more consistently positive experiences. This one was an anomaly; however if something similar happens at a different location, my opinion may begin to change. This experience underscores the need for consistency in training, performance, monitoring and coaching. It clearly shows how even one or two individuals can influence an entire experience and the customers' perception of a single location or an entire brand.

This next example illustrates the importance of consistency in delivering a superior experience at every customer point of interaction each and every time. Consistency starts at the top with well-defined culture, process and systems. Finally, it becomes all about YOU–who knew? Let's look at six steps that can help define and refine the process and systems that make an exceptional customer experience at every point of interaction.

1. Identify existing points of interactions that influence your experience. Answer questions like these, candidly, and then ask every person to do the same.

   - List every point of interaction our customers have with humans, our facility and our materials. Are these points of interaction consistent? What's different?

   - What is the existing process from the first contact to last contact with a customer?

   - How are the customer relationships maintained, and what points of interaction are used in this process?

   - Who touches the customer by design, and how?

   - Does every person understand the brand identity and customer experience the business is striving to create?

   - How is this communicated?

- What do your customers tell you about their experiences?
- Do you have a telephone system that prevents personal interaction?
- Evaluate the quality and consistency of the existing points of interaction by asking:
- What do they want from our business and in every experience with us?
- What do our customers need from our business and our people?
- What do they desire from every point of interaction with us?
- What do they value from businesses and people like ours?
- Knowing this, where do we excel at meeting these?
- What is our performance average?
- Are we consistent at every point of interaction?
- Where must we improve?

2. Imagine what a new, improved or expanded customer experience would be like if there were no limitations.
   - How would we as a business deliver an exceptional customer experience if there were no limits in terms of resources, locations, technology and funding?
   - How would each person do the same?

- How would existing points of interaction be improved or changed?
- Would any points of interaction be eliminated?
- What new points of interaction would you envision?

3. Once imagined, define the new experiences, refinements and changes and their points of interaction.

   - Establish systems and processes.
   - Set baseline standards – the minimum every person must meet every time.
   - Capture best practices – above and beyond the minimum – and share with other people.

4. Communicate, implement and measure.

5. Is it working?

   - What can we do better?
   - Is it personal? Do you have someone who can answer the phone knowledgeably?

6. Technology

   - Look at existing technology and make sure it complements and supports personal relationships with customers and enhances the customer experience.
   - What happens when the Internet, electricity or computer systems go down? Are there back-ups? Can you still serve the customer? If not, look for new technology to fill these gaps.

- Is technology in place to capture customer information simply and transparently?
- Does technology improve responsiveness and accessibility to people and the business?
- Is the website effective in communicating the brand? Is it easy to navigate, and does it provide the information customers need, want and desire?
- Do the people in the business understand the best way to use technology?

While consistency starts at the top with management and the right processes and systems, there is one essential element that can make a point of interaction positive or negative, which can build a loyal client or turn a buyer into a shopper and can reinforce the brand in a positive way or tarnish it for an unknown period of time. That one essential element is YOU.

The best management, the best systems, processes and practices in the world are only as effective as the people on the front line, those who actually touch the customer, who care. In other words, you. Your success is gained and lost by your attitude.

Picture a typical gas gauge on a car. Generally, there is an E for EMPTY on the left and an F for FULL on the right with an arc connecting the two and hash marks indicating each quarter of the tank. If you are trying to drive from Los Angeles to San Francisco and you can only use the gas already in the tank, how far will you get on a tank that's half-full? You might make about half way or perhaps a little further, depending on the car's miles per gallon performance. If you want to arrive in San Francisco, you better have a full tank.

The same is true in delivering an exceptional customer experience. It is like the right side of the tank is positive and the left is negative. Each day, every person prepares themselves on how they intend to approach their day. They can get up and embrace the day with a positive attitude, FULL tank, or grumble about the awful day ahead with a negative attitude or EMPTY tank. In either case, the attitude determines the outcome. The same about attitude is made at every customer point of interaction. With a FULL tank or positive attitude, the customer experience is sure to be remarkable. Focusing on the negative – lower sales, higher overhead, problems with a coworker or even a "bad morning" – shifts attitudes, depletes the tank and negatively impacts the customer experience. If you approach with a negative mindset, YOU lose. It's all in the way you approach it.

Maintaining a positive attitude is a choice. And it is the first step in creating a positive customer experience. So, before you interact, check your gas gauge. Do you have a FULL tank? If not, change your attitude. Forgetting once is a mistake; after that, it is a decision.

Brands and businesses live or die through customer experiences. Whether intentional or not, each time a customer, or even an employee, interacts with your brand, an impression is made. Unfortunately, an inconsistent experience can be devastating. The ultimate goal, what all brands seek, is consistency of experience. The only way to deliver a consistent experience is from the top down, from management to processes and systems and finally, to YOU. Who knew?

"Your job is NOT to sell,
but to help customers buy."

It's All About You!

CHAPTER 3

Just Do Your Job

NIKE HAD IT right when they coined the slogan, "Just Do It." And if people today simply focused on just doing the best job possible, client loyalty would never be in question. It is like New England Patriots' coach Bill Belichick said, "Just do your job – well." Yet every day, people don't deliver. Why? While there are several barriers to success, the three most prevalent are an understanding of the job, fear and attitude.

First things first: Your job is NOT to sell, but to help customers buy. Virtually everyone in business today would stop reading here to take exception to this statement. Yet, it's a core truth of our profession. So again, what is your job, if not to sell?

It is to help customers find the exact product or service that meets their needs, wants and desires, and, in doing so, make sure their experience is positive.

To succeed in this, three things must happen every day, all day. You must be 100% in the game and ready to work with a single-minded focus for each client. You must ask the right questions, actively listen, learn and understand problems from their customers' points-of-view, so you can guide their selection. Finally, you must help customers "fall in love" with the product or service by showing how it improves their lives – either personally or professionally.

Fear of failure, breaking the rules or losing a job will stop anyone, no matter how good they are, from success. Fear typically comes from a culture that does not empower its professionals to succeed, to act in the best interest of the client.

Someone we know had decided to rejoin a gym after only a brief three month hiatus. Instead of welcoming the person back and doing everything possible to waive the hefty "new member" fee, the representative said that fees were set by the corporate office and that there was no choice but to charge her, regardless of how little time she had been gone. She left, uncertain of her next step. She did not understand that membership or subscription based businesses must charge fees like this to prevent people from jumping from business to business every time a special offer is available. These businesses earn their money on monthly subscriptions. When members hopscotch from gym to gym, in order for them to manage the business, they need to have an idea of projected income. Managing financially can be impossible. The next day, the lady returned and talked to another employee. This employee reiterated the corporate policy but then looked at every possible option and type of membership, not simply the one she had been told to "push." She succeeded in helping the customer select a membership option that because she paid 100% up front, essentially eliminated the new member fee, provided several complimentary services and cost less per month than her previous membership. In the long run, she paid less money, but she had to pay it all up front.

The first person worked from a place of fear of breaking the corporate policy. This person did not believe she was empowered to do anything but provide quotes on the current membership special and the deal she was told she should be pushing. As a result, she failed to build trust, failed to positively represent the brand and failed to gain a customer. This person needs to follow the advice from a well-known advertising campaign, "Try it. You'll like it."

The second employee adopted the Nike approach, "Just Do It." She focused on doing her job—helping the client find the right product for her needs, wants and desires—and succeeded in all areas where the first employee failed.

Let's talk about empowerment as a means of eliminating fear because without empowerment, almost all we have is fear. Do you know what you are empowered to do?

Empowerment is the process where people enable themselves to take action, control work and make decisions independently. Empowerment comes from the individual. It is not something that comes from a manager. Consequently, people wait to be empowered while managers wonder why they don't just do what is best for clients. The only obligation an organization has to its employees is to create a positive work environment and remove barriers so they are encouraged to act in empowered ways.

Previously, I shared several positive anecdotes that exemplified people who embraced empowerment.

- The Macy's worker made the decision to put client service first, found the apron and personally contacted the client to make sure it was delivered.
- The bookstore representative made the decision to find a solution, even if it meant buying the book from the competition to meet the needs of the client.

These examples of empowered behavior lead us directly to attitude because without the proper attitude, no one will ever embrace empowerment. Again, what are you empowered to do? Do you take advantage of your empowerment to deliver the best customer experience?

Every day, in every situation, every individual has a choice when it comes to embracing a positive or negative attitude. And in every instance, the attitude a person chooses becomes reality. In sales, a positive attitude drives the ability to do the best job possible. It drives willingness to make empowered choices. It drives the ability to help clients find the right product or service that specifically meets or exceeds their unique situation.

Consider this story. Years ago, there was a man who sold hot dogs. He didn't listen to the radio, watch TV or read the paper. He simply sold hot dogs. He put up signs telling how good they were. He stood on the side of the road and cried, "Buy a hot dog, mister?" And people bought because he was so enthusiastic. And his business grew. One day, his son came to help him out. His son said, "Haven't you heard? The economy is in terrible shape!" The father thought, my son's been to college, he reads the newspaper, he listens to the radio and he ought to know. So, he cut down on his meat and bun orders, took down his advertising signs and no longer bothered to call out to sell his hot dogs. And his sales fell—virtually overnight. His conclusion—my son was right, we are in a depression.

In reality, the man's attitude changed. As long as he kept a positive attitude, the world around him didn't matter, he prospered.

Your Job Is To Help the Customer **Buy**

The ability to be positive at all times is the one thing that will ensure you're a winner in the end. When you are positive, people will find you irresistible. People will remember you not for how you handled life, but for how you made others feel. A positive attitude fosters creative thinking, which is a critical attribute in embracing empowerment. In every situation, people should THINK – Transform, Help, Improve, Notice and Know.

- Look for ways to **Transform** the client experience, so it is memorable and positive.
- Do everything possible to **Help** resolve issues and meet the client's needs, wants and desires.
- Find ways to **Improve** your own skills by listening, learning and acting.
- **Notice** the little things you can do to make a difference, from wiping the restroom counter before you leave, to providing water to clients as they shop.
- Get to **Know** your clients. Build relationships. Call them by name. Anticipate their needs.

Your attitude and your ability to have a positive influence on the attitudes of others will affect not only your sales, but every area of your life. Nothing in your life will pay more rewards than your ability to have and maintain a great attitude.

There is a song by the group the American Authors called "Best Day of My Life." A colleague of mine told me that one day recently, she woke up and the lyric, "This is gonna be the best day of my life…" was going through her head. It was the only part of the song she knew, but it made her feel so positive as she woke, that it became her mantra for the day. Turned out, it was a pretty great day. Like my colleague, when you get up each morning you have a choice – be positive or negative. Find your mantra – a song, a phrase, a poem, a verse – then say it, repeat it and come to believe it.

So how do you start to "Just Do It"?

1. Get up every day and make a decision to embrace a positive attitude, to focus on what you want and what your customers want. Think about it, visualize it and say it over and over. More important than the words you say to others are the words you say to yourself. It can mean the difference between a bad day and a good day – at work.

2. Be conscious or aware of your words and thoughts. Focus on what you can control, not on what you can't control. Practice catching yourself when your thoughts, actions and words are negative; stop and make an immediate change. Catch yourself succeeding and celebrate these successes, no matter how small.

3. Write down what you want specifically. Make a contract with yourself. Picture it in your mind. Once you see it clearly, you can move toward it. Practice. Practice. Practice.

Small successes and large achievements start the same way. Focusing on what you want, helps you make it happen, for yourself and for your customers. You may not win every sale, but if you can honestly say you did everything possible to satisfy the customer, then you won in the long term.

Every day, say to yourself, "My job is to help my customers buy." Every day, embrace an empowered work style. Even within the company processes or rules, everyone has the ability and opportunity to act empowered to help clients. The examples shared previously are proof. Every day and in every situation—from lousy traffic and slow service, to unexpected problems and disappointing news—everyone can choose whether or not it's a good or bad day.

By making the right choices every day, doing your job becomes easy and more rewarding.

It's All About You!

CHAPTER 4

Most People Don't Listen

IN BUSINESS, ONE vital key to success is to listen, listen some more and then to keep listening. Too often, people talk more than they listen and pitch products or services without clearly learning about the needs, wants and desires of their customers. A good business person listens to what the client says before making recommendations. For example, initial appearances might not reveal that a young couple is looking for a larger vehicle before starting a family, or that a young adult might be looking for a top-of-the-line luxury vehicle.

It's important to clearly define what we mean by needs, wants and desires. A need is something you must have, something that is absolutely necessary to survive in a given situation. A want is something you would like to have, something that would make a situation better than simply survival. A desire is similar to a want, but amplified by strong emotional feelings for comfort, luxury, status and more.

Let's look at examples for all three categories.

Item	Need	Want	Desire
Clothing	A pair of inexpensive or used jeans and a T-shirt meet the need for clothing.	A brand name, like Guess, meets the want to be associated with the attributes of that brand.	The newest jeans, straight from a designer at Fashion Week, fill the desire to appear important.
Transportation	A bus meets the need of basic transportation.	A car delivers on the want for speed and comfort.	A luxury car or sports car meets the desire to portray a specific image.
Food	A meal.	A Happy Meal meets the want to feed and entertain the kids.	A meal from a five star restaurant meets the desire to partake of the finest experience.
Communication	A $39.00 flip phone.	A smart phone.	The latest technology to debut.

In business, it is important to distinguish these three factors and to guide customers in making a selection that meets all of them. When this happens, customers reach the point of "falling in love" with the product or service. Other factors, like price or delivery times, no longer matter.

Consider this. If a person goes to visit an eye doctor, what do they want? If you answered glasses, you are wrong. If you answered that the person wants to see better, you are correct. People seek out eye doctors because they have a vision problem. They don't go to get glasses. In fact, they hope they don't need glasses. They go because they want to have better vision.

This is the difference between understanding a customer's needs, wants and desires and assuming that a customer wants a product or service. The only way to develop this understanding is through active listening.

Business people are like investigators. They need to ask questions that move the sale forward, yet often when people talk to each other, they don't listen closely. Salespeople can be easily and often distracted, half-listening and half-thinking about something else, especially with cell phones and wearable technology constantly vibrating, ringing and pinging. When they are focused more on the sale than on the customer, they are often busy formulating a response to what is being said or silently rehearsing their pitch instead of listening. They assume that they have heard what their clients are saying many times before, so rather than paying attention and focusing on their customers, they focus on how they can close a sale. Often, they answer a question before a customer finishes asking it, and typically, they give the wrong answer.

Listen, listen, listen. Active listening encourages silence. By waiting several seconds to respond to customers, you make customers feel heard, which in turn, makes them feel more comfortable. Although many find the conscious effort to stay quiet challenging, silence creates the space that will prompt customers to share additional information. It also provides time, so you can respond thoughtfully and intelligently to the customers' specific needs. Ask customers if they mind if you take notes. Think about how this makes them feel. It communicates that you believe what they are saying is important, that it matters. It builds confidence and trust. As you take notes, ask probing questions. Often, questions will come to you during the conversation, but it is best to be prepared with questions based on previous experiences. However, before using prepared questions, be sure they are relevant.

Make customers feel heard. Clarify what they've said. Rephrase their comments or questions in your own words to ensure that you heard and understood. You might say:

- "What I am hearing is…"
- "Help me understand…"
- "Tell me more…"

Listen for what customers don't say, but imply. What customers fail to include is often more important than what is stated. Look for clues as to what they really mean, what concerns customers may have, what is important to them, what they value and what they need, want and desire. Only then will you be able to do your job—helping customers find the exact product or service that meets their needs, wants and desires through a positive experience.

Here are six common sense rules for active listening:

1. **Slow down.** People tend to be very talkative. They have lots of ideas and opinions, characteristics that are important, but that can also lead to talking so fast it's impossible to keep up. Talking quickly can only hurt the relationship with a customer. They'll either lose interest or become uncomfortable and want to leave. Instead, speak at a measured pace. Pause in case customers need clarification. Ask questions to guide and help shape what they share.

2. **Never interrupt.** Interrupting is rude and can be interpreted as condescending. And it's a clear indication that you are not genuinely interested in what customers are saying. Even worse, it usually means that you miss out on something interesting your customers would have said if they had had the chance. They might have had other things to share that would help shape your conversation, but they couldn't because you interjected. Often, interruption is caused by a fear of silence, of the empty space that borders on awkwardness. Get over it! In fact, embrace it. More often than not, when you pause after customers finish talking, they will fill the silence by finding something else to add. It's often these additional bits of information that are the most valuable.

   The only time it's appropriate to interrupt is when you didn't hear something. Even if you want to clarify something that was said, make a note and come back to it when the customer has finished speaking.

3. **Clarify and restate.** A big part of listening closely to someone is letting them know you understand what they are saying. Clarifying and restating the conversation not only ensures you have the right information, but also lets customers know that you're listening. When this happens, customers often show their appreciation by sharing even more details. And they will find you likable, which is important in establishing a relationship. Try paraphrasing customers' thoughts in your own words make sure you understood and to show them the you care about what they're saying. This avoids miscommunication that can cause harm to your rapport later on. Don't let important information get lost in translation. Use words like, "If I understand you correctly…" or "I want to be sure I am hearing you…" or "To put it another way,…" These lead-ins give customers a heads-up that you are trying to clarify meaning and cues them to listen closely.

4. **Listen to emotions.** Words are not always an accurate representation of what people feel. It can be hard to interpret conversations, especially if they are being conducted via telephone because you lose the ability to read a person's body language. Even so, using audio clues, it is possible to come close to an accurate interpretation. Start by feeling out

their tone of voice and stress levels. Practice during conversations with coworkers and learn to recognize how the volume, speed and tone of voice indicate how people feel. In every sales situation, make it a goal to think about what the person might be thinking and feeling behind their words. I call this listening between the lines.

5. **Be an active listener.** Listen with your entire body and with genuine interest. Be fascinated in what customers tell you. Sit on the edge of your chair, literally, and listen intently. Likewise, be aware of customers' body language. Notice how customers are standing or sitting. Are their arms crossed? Are they leaning forward or back? Customers who are interested may lean forward with arms uncrossed, showing they are open to what is being said. Customers who have crossed arms or legs might be indicating that they still are not fully embracing the messages. When meeting with customers, try to position yourself at about a 45-degree angle, so that you are leaning in toward them as you speak. If you can, position yourself so that your feet are pointing at the customers. Leaning in and directing your body towards customers shows that you are fully focused on them.

6. **Make eye contact.** Customers are unlikely to trust a salesperson that cannot make eye contact. There is no need to look directly in the eyes of customers

every moment they are speaking or every time that you speak, but keeping a consistent amount of eye contact shows that you have nothing to hide. If looking into customers' eyes feels awkward, look just above them at the forehead. From their perspective, it still seems as if you are looking at them.

> *It's essential to know customers' needs, wants and desires and help guide them in the right direction.*

Listening is a learned and practiced skill that will help build trust and confidence. It is the first step in building relationships. Listening and learning from customers takes a concerted effort that becomes easier with practice. It also involves giving cues to customers that show you are listening intently and care about what they say. When people listen, they can more easily put themselves in their customers' shoes, empathize and be sympathetic. Actively listening will help you understand that sometimes a problem isn't a problem until you make it one.

Who knew? Understanding what customers want starts with you. By asking the right questions, using common sense, listening actively and being mindful of body language, you will discover important information that will help you guide customers as they make their purchasing decisions.

It's All About You!

CHAPTER 5

Put Yourself in Your Clients Place

PARAPHRASING MARK TWAIN, a famous American philosopher and author, "If common sense was common, it wouldn't be common anymore." Everything we do in life comes down to a common sense approach. The basic tenants of sales, the "common sense" of business, have not changed much in nearly 150 years.

Mark Twain wrote one of the first sales training manuals that existed. He understood and appreciated the value of a process. His 1865 manual, *The Successful Sales Agent*, helped him sell thousands of copies of *Huck Finn* and *Tom Sawyer* through "subscription agents," people who would pre-sell his books door-to-door using sample pages of the books.

Mark Twain opened his manual by saying, "You must be interested yourself, or you cannot interest others; and the way for you to become interested, is to know your book thoroughly." This remains a basic truth today. Like Twain states, a business must have a clear understanding of and commitment to delivering on its mission, as well as an in-depth knowledge of its customers. Likewise, its people must have an exhaustive knowledge about the company they work for, its products and services and its customers in order to, as Twain says, "Interest others."

While a bit disparaging to the human spirit, this sentiment has been echoed by philosophers throughout time, from Voltaire's "Common sense is not so common," to Philip Dormer Stanhope's "Common sense is the best sense I know of: abide by it; it will counsel you best," and many others. And it remains true in the world of sales.

The majority of what transpires in a successful business transaction is just that – common sense – and it always will be. No silver bullet or magic technology can ever replace the ability of people to put themselves in their customers' places. Yet repeatedly, businesses and individuals try to change effective concepts and practices, and in the process, they lose sight of their original goals and of what their customers are seeking. Common sense dictates that businesses and their people listen, develop empathy, understand their customers' needs, wants and desires, and establish relationships. Only then can they help customers find the right solution.

Again, citing Mark Twain, "Supposing is good, but knowing is better." All successful business practices start with knowing customers today and as they change over time. Common sense, yes; the business norm, rarely. One of the best known examples of businesses that failed because they neglected to understand how their customers' needs, wants and desires changed is Eastman Kodak. According to *U.S. News and World Report*, for nearly a century, no company in the camera market could touch Kodak's success. The company's historic breakthroughs in photography included the Brownie camera in 1900, Kodachrome color film, the handheld movie camera and the easy-load Instamatic camera. But Kodak's stellar rise ended with the advent of digital photography and the associated printers, software, file sharing and third-party apps that developed in tandem, even though their scientists invented the digital camera. Kodak failed to believe consumers would embrace these technologies, and years later, when Kodak tried to reshape its business, the magic never returned.

Today, Kodak is a non-descript technology company whose corporate description doesn't even mention photography: "Kodak is poised to take advantage of the digital transition under way in packaging markets; the growing demand for graphic communications around the world, especially in emerging markets; and dynamic growth in the market for printed electronics, sensors, fuel cells and other printed products with functions beyond visual communications."

Similarly, according to the same *U.S. News and World Report* article, Blockbuster, while surviving the transition from VHS to DVD, failed to adapt to changes in its customers' behavior. The company ignored new formats for video delivery from mail to streaming. When it did introduce delivery by mail, it was too late. Seemingly overnight Blockbuster found itself chasing an industry it had helped create. Despite its acquisition by Dish Network, Blockbuster discontinued its DVD-by-mail service and closed its remaining 300 stores. *Bloomberg Business* reported that this move was, "ending an era for a chain that was once a ubiquitous part of American shopping centers." Blockbuster's biggest competitor, Netflix, succeeded in sending videos through the mail, embraced video-on-demand and streaming and is now one of the premier content-on-demand companies.

These are two highly visible cases. However, there are hundreds or thousands more where thriving businesses failed to keep connected to their customers and, as a result, drove their own demise. On the other hand, some companies work diligently to listen to their customers and think out of the box to anticipate and meet their changing needs without losing their core focus.

One business that mastered this art is Petco, which was originally established as a large, warehouse style retail store with products for all types of animals. By focusing on the needs, wants and desires of pet owners, executives realized that there was a large population of dog and cat owners who desired a smaller store with more personal service and upscale, unique offerings. The company launched a new brand concept, Unleashed by Petco, in the midst of a recession without losing sight of their original mission and vision. The new, complementary brand addressed the needs of a large group of underserved pet owners. Many pundits wrongly assumed Unleashed by Petco's sales would cannibalize Petco's revenues, yet the company's sales grew consistently from $2.7 billion when Unleashed by Petco was introduced, to $3.2 billion in four years, according to *Forbes*.

- Petco is described as "a leading pet specialty retailer that focuses on nurturing powerful relationships between people and pets…by providing the products, services, advice and experiences that keep pets physically fit, mentally alert, socially engaged and emotionally happy. Everything we do is guided by our vision for Healthier Pets. Happier People. Better World."

- The new brand, Unleashed by Petco, is "a smaller format neighborhood store that provides an ideal environment for increased community interactions and extends Petco's involvement in local animal-welfare efforts and community events. [The store] provides a tailored assortment of mostly dog and cat products focused on natural foods and 'Made in the USA' brands. Unleashed by Petco also offers a variety of services including dog training, vaccination clinics and pet parties, as well as grooming and self-service pet washing at select locations."

While most companies focus specifically on customers, Petco is also concerned about its impact on society because that's what its customers want and what they care about. While providing quality products, information and advice, it also addresses important issues related to animals in society through its foundation fundraising programs, youth education and a commitment to organic, natural and American-made products. In 2011, Petco changed its tagline to read, "Where the healthy pets go," to emphasize its "commitment to helping pets live the healthiest and longest lives possible."

A business case study published by the University of New Mexico states that Petco, "adopted the perspective of a subset of customers and found a new way to meet their needs without losing the premise of their overall business."

Finally, an MIT Sloan Management comparison of Whole Foods and Trader Joe's revealed some interesting insights on two very different but successful approaches to creating customer experiences. Even though both stores are known for healthy choices and unique foods, their customer experiences are very different and specifically designed to meet the needs of their unique customers.

The original premise behind Trader Joe's was that going to the grocery store should be an authentically enjoyable customer experience. The founder achieved this vision by worker adjustments, process redesigns and physical changes to the store atmosphere. Employees wear Aloha shirts, product returns are welcome at all times and the employees are always eager to help customers find products. Small kitchens cook up treats and provide recipes with ingredients that can be found easily in coolers next to the demo kitchen. A ship's bell replaces the use of an intercom, and hand-painted signs and wood-paneled walls further promote a "getaway" feeling. To speed up the check-out process, all products are sold as units (rather than by weight), and the use of conveyor belts and special lines is virtually non-existent.

Whole Foods is committed to ensuring each customer has a positive experience and feels good about their shopping experience, despite higher prices. They appeal to customers' senses: sight, smell and taste. From customers' first moments in the store, they are greeted by the brightly colored display of fresh fruits and vegetables. As they walk the aisles, they encounter opportunities to taste a variety of food samples. In many stores, the smells of the buffet-style, self-serve department entice customers to grab food to go or a bite to eat at the tables in the store. Throughout their experience, customers encounter knowledgeable specialists who are eager to advise them on the best cheese or the perfect slice of meat. Whole Foods believes that this level of expertise is essential to achieving their goal of providing excellent customer service. At the checkout, it is Whole Foods' attention to details that sets it apart. For example, if a customer is buying a carton of eggs, the cashier opens them to make sure that none are cracked and places tape or rubber bands around the containers to secure them. These small gestures go a long way in making customers feel that they are getting superior treatment and value.

With all four of these companies, regardless of who walks into a store, the brand is consistent and easily recognizable. The customer experience distinctly demonstrates that each brand and its sales professionals have a clear understanding of to whom they are selling. While these businesses are plainly superior, the epitome of a consistent brand and exceptional customer experience may be Demoulas Market Basket.

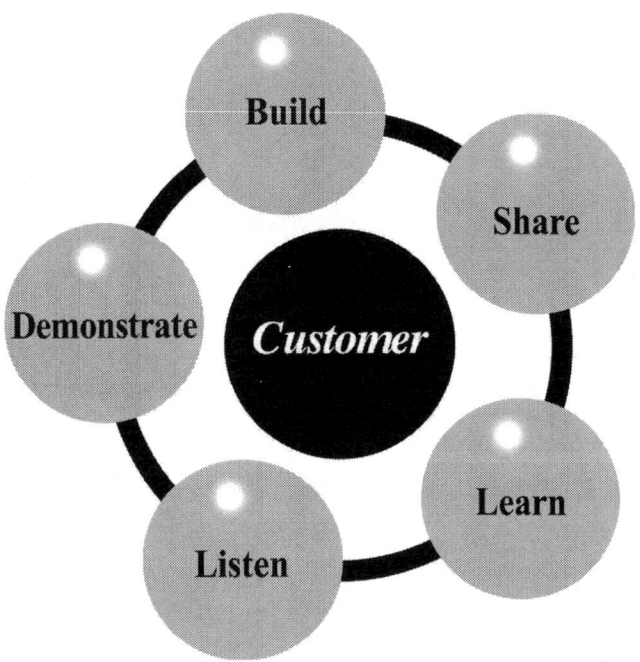

In 1917, Greek immigrants Athanasios ("Arthur") and Efrosini Demoulas opened DeMoulas Market, a grocery store in the Acre neighborhood of Lowell, Massachusetts, that specialized in fresh lamb. After a rocky start, the business, run by two of the founders' sons, thrived. By the 1970's it had become a modern supermarket chain of 15 stores, despite in-fighting by family members. In 2008, Arthur T. Demoulas was named president. He was known for his ability to remember his associates' names, birthdays and milestones, attending many of their weddings and funerals, checking in on ill employees and asking about the spouses and children of his workers. He was seen as a father figure by a number of his employees and compared to *It's a Wonderful Life* protagonist George Bailey for his willingness to put people over profit.

Family disputes continued and on June 23, 2014, Arthur T. Demoulas was fired by the board. In response, six high-level managers resigned and 300 employees held a rally outside Market Basket's Chelsea, Massachusetts, flagship store on June 24. Additional protests with as many as 5,000 employees *and customers* were held at the company's Tewksbury headquarters and other locations demanding the reinstatement of Arthur T. Many warehouse and corporate office workers, including delivery truck drivers, went on strike, leaving some shelves bare at many Market Basket locations. In the midst of the protests, Arthur T. offered to buy the entire company from his cousins, an offer that the board ultimately accepted. Today, the chain continues to thrive with the support of loyal employees. Market Basket's starting wages for full-time clerks are above minimum wage, and employees who work more than 1,000 hours a year are eligible to enter the profit-sharing program. Employees also receive benefits, including healthcare and paid sick leave. Market Basket does not have self-checkout lanes. Company

President Arthur T. Demoulas stated that he wanted, "a human being waiting on a human being."

What makes this story unique is that it was the first time that customers protested a management change. How did this happen? Arthur T. put people before profits and wanted people to help people.

No business or store is exempt from the need to consistently uphold its brand with exceptional customer service. Think for a moment. When was the last time you visited a store or called a business about a product or service and walked away empty-handed? It almost never happens, and if it does, then the business had better know why.

This caliber of attention to and understanding of the customer is critical on a personal level for every person. Customers seek out specialists, knowledgeable individuals who listen, learn and then help them buy.

Everyone in a business must be a specialist—a selection specialist—who goes out of their way to show a customer all the reasons they should buy, reasons that align with the customers' needs, wants and desires. Period. If that means spending an hour with a customer when your colleagues spend 15 minutes, so be it. Will it work every time? No. But *your* name will be the one that customers remember and recommend to their friends and family.

If you are buying a house, you don't care about the square footage of the kitchen. You care about making your family dinner and having room to eat together, or a space where you can make and enjoy coffee each morning. A good realtor, a selection specialist, will know exactly how to help a customer picture these scenes, so they begin to feel at home.

It's called good business and it encompasses all these behaviors:

- Enthusiasm
- Conviction
- Imagination
- Courtesy
- Honesty
- Desire
- Self-discipline
- Faith
- Courage
- Goals

- Service
- Organization
- Motivation
- Personality
- Work
- Product knowledge
- Personal appearance
- Self-confidence
- Perseverance
- Showmanship

As a selection specialist, you should use these traits to build value for your product and services in the hearts and minds of your customers. Give your customers what they want and build their trust, so that they understand that whenever they need the product or service being sold, you are the go-to person.

Who knew? Understanding the customers' perspectives, thinking outside the box without compromising the goal, and building the salesmanship skills, all starts with you.

———

"Sometimes first impressions are created before you ever meet a customer."

———

It's All About You!

CHAPTER 6

First Impressions Aren't Everything

THERE IS A difference between having a job and going to work. A job is something you have to do, and it's usually not a lot of fun. Going to work, however, can be enjoyable and fun. It's your responsibility to be part of that fun. When you do, who benefits? Everyone.

Is your job about business, profitability, a paycheck or a commission? No. It's about people. Period. Human nature dictates that we approach others and situations with a positive attitude; customers approach employees with a sense of belief and trust. Their first impression can reinforce that belief or change it from a positive to a negative. Your job is to make a lasting, positive impression.

The challenge is that first impressions are often formed well before you ever encounter a customer. They can be formed through observation and experience, and they can change instantly. A business might be located in a beautiful building, with professional décor and extra amenities like a coffee bar, free Wi-Fi, etc., creating a positive first impression. Yet when the first person a customer encounters is dressed in an unprofessional manner, maybe in shorts and a T-shirt, that impression can quickly change. Conversely, we've seen people do exceptionally well working from trailers while a business is undergoing construction. The building doesn't matter. You do. What would you think if you went into a pristinely clean doctor's office or hospital and were greeted by a physician in a torn, dirty lab coat? Your first impression (the surroundings) and your second impression (the individual) create a disconnect that built fear, uncertainty and doubt about the consistency and quality of care and service.

In a world of automated responses, Internet access, social media and instant communication, the term "first impression" has a new meaning. First impressions are malleable; they can be created and recreated, reinforced or diminished several times before solidifying into a clear "first impression." However, when they are solidified, they are lasting and extremely difficult to change. That's why it's critical that the image a business portrays be consistent across every part of a company.

Consider these factors that create or alter a first impression well before a customer ever encounters anyone in a business.

To create or reinforce a positive first impression, a business should have...

- ...an easily navigated website that is optimized for mobile devices, provides the information customers seek and aligns with the brand and values of the business.

- ...advertisements and collateral, which mirror the brand and company's values while providing clear, concise and correct information.

- ...a human answering phone calls, or if automated, an easily navigated system that avoids repetition and delivers a positive experience.

- ...a friendly environment that instantly communicates the brand and values, from parking lots, the building and awnings, to clean floors and the receptionist or greeter. Is the parking lot accessible to customers, are there special parking spaces that meet customers' unique needs, e.g. "to-go" customers, families, expectant moms or electric vehicles?

- ...nametags and uniform dress for all employees so that they are easily identifiable and approachable. These help break down barriers to communication and create an impression that the employees want to engage with and help customers.

- …special "extras" that cater to customers' needs and make it easy for them to do business with you. For example, many grocery stores have carts for children to use, so they can shop with their parents. These stores also put items that children want at their eye level, which generally increases sales.

Disney has mastered the art of creating and maintaining positive first impressions. That's why it really is the happiest place on earth. Even before you visit, they make it easy with an intuitive and straightforward website. From the second you enter the property, there are greeters who smile and offer to help with parking, maps, directions and information. If you want to know the time of the next parade, they know it without fail. And when you are leaving, if you can't find your car, they can direct you to the exact row where you parked simply by knowing the time you arrived. At Disneyland, the buildings are designed to create a magical impression. Despite being at the end of the street, the castle looks huge, which defies the laws of perspective. Why? Each building is designed and built at a slight incline to create this unique impression. As you walk down Main Street, you will rarely see any trash, despite thousands of visitors. You enjoy a sensory experience of sights, sounds and smells. Scents of chocolate and popcorn are infused purposely in the air. Signs show waiting times for rides to alleviate the frustration of waiting without information, and FastPass options put guests in control of their day.

First impressions are time-based. In fact, they are very much like a dating relationship. All the positives, the benefits and best qualities are the first to appear. Over time, something negative might happen that causes these positive first impressions to diminish and become negative. In business, this can happen in a matter of seconds.

It would be rare to find anyone who has not met someone, talked to them for a few seconds and decided that they probably didn't like them or want to deal with them. Yet how many have continued the conversation only to have this initial impression change? For example, reaching a telephone customer service representative who was difficult to understand, who used technical jargon or who seemed to talk down to the customer may have created an immediate negative impression. As the conversation progressed and the customer service representative gained an understanding of how best to communicate by listening to the caller, altered their approach and delivered a positive experience, the customer's impression changed. Technically, the first impression did not change, but a new, more powerful and lasting impression was formed as time went on.

Everyone in business has this opportunity and ability throughout every interaction. The key is to recognize when the first impression may not be positive and then to quickly do something to change it.

Earlier, it was noted that positive or negative first impressions can be created before ever talking to or meeting a representative of a business. Often, when people have a problem, complaint or concern, they can be irrational. They don't think about the reason behind a problem. They don't focus on the positive outcomes. Instead, they react and vent their anger on the messenger, so to speak, not only for the situation, but for whatever downside to the solution exists.

This can catch employees off guard, especially when the negative situation was set in motion before they encounter a customer. Yet in every situation, the person has the ability to recreate the impression in a positive way. Let's examine two situations.

- A bank customer opens her bank statement and sees a $15.00 charge for being under the daily balance, even though she was only below the limit for a day. Before ever picking up the phone to call, a negative impression is formed and the customer is – to say the least – upset. The person who answers the phone has no idea that they are about to face an angry customer. When this happens, the bank representative has two choices: exacerbate the situation or change the negative impression. The bank representative can remind the customer that when the account was opened, the terms and conditions were clearly explained, although this will only worsen the situation. Or the representative can empathize, apologize for the inconvenience, waive the fee and then gently remind the customer of the agreement, so there is no surprise in the future. By offering options, the representative can take a negative and convert it to a positive.

- A cable customer calls to report poor quality or an outage. The caller is greeted with an automated phone system with instructions like, "Press one for this and two for that. Enter your account number, phone number, address, etc." Already frustrated before making the call, this system adds to the customer's aggravation. By the time a human is reached, the customer is not happy. When the representative asks the customer to repeat the information already entered or transfers them from place to place, the customer often reaches a boiling point. At some point, the customer is ready to say, "If you say you want to transfer me again, I am going to reach through the phone and take you with me." Again, there are two options here. The customer could be abruptly transferred again, or the representative could empathize, tell them they understand how frustrating it can be, and stay on the line with them until they are connected to and introduced to the right person.

People have choices. They can fire you at any time and go to your competition. Everyone has always had options, and today more choices exist than ever before. In each of these situations, the representative who finally talks to the customer has the potential to make the situation better, or worse, depending on the approach taken. The person can follow a prepared script and put the responsibility back on the customer or empathize, make the customer feel like he is being heard and find a solution.

Every employee's job is to create a positive impression for themselves in the minds and hearts of every customer. Regardless of the impression a customer may have of the company or of those previously spoken to, every person has the opportunity to create a new first impression and to improve the lasting impression for the company with every customer interaction. It doesn't matter if it's on the phone, meeting a customer face to face or chatting. It doesn't matter what industry a business is in, retail or business-to-business, technology, food service, clothing, automotive or travel.

> ## A first impression doesn't have to be the last impression.

Like every professional, you face the challenge of not knowing what happened before you reach the customer. Even so, this shouldn't matter if every interaction is approached with empathy and a sincere desire to help, as in this example.

A passenger on Alaska Airlines had planned a trip for her birthday, but a bad case of the flu forced her to cancel. When she called to cancel, she explained to the representative that she was sick and acknowledged that she was responsible for the hefty cancellation fee. The representative empathized, telling her it was truly a shame that she was sick and couldn't fly. Engaged with the representative, she said that it was especially lousy since it was her birthday. The representative briefly put her on hold to take care of the cancellation. When she returned, she said that she had talked to her boss and secured a full credit – no cancellation fee. She then wished her a happy birthday. By listening, engaging and empathizing, this representative exceeded expectations and created a lasting superior impression. As a result, this traveler has not stopped talking about the great service provided by the company.

First impressions can become lasting impressions. Lasting impressions can change. Businesses and every employee working for them must be prepared to do business in a positive consistent manner that reflects the image of the company and that engages with customers. First impressions are formed again and again, each time a customer encounters someone new. By actively listening, developing and exhibiting empathy, working to solve problems and looking at things from the customer's point of view, every business can form a positive lasting impression.

"Listen."

It's All About You!

CHAPTER 7

Find a Solution

WHAT'S YOUR EXCUSE? If you say, "It's the way we do it," or "It is policy," then that's exactly what it is, an excuse. Putting the customer first is the mantra of every business. It must also be your mantra. What do you need to do to put the customer first, to delight the customer and meet their needs, wants and desires in a project or service? It's always best to "ask for forgiveness rather than for permission." This is critical if you intend to make decisions and find solutions that benefit the customer. Following this adage not only puts the customer first, it puts the business and ultimately yourself first. It is the best decision you can make, even if it is outside the box and your comfort zone, and even if it's a mistake. As long as it benefits the customer and the business, do it. Yet this almost never happens. Why?

Most people in business, and even in life, are either afraid to break the rules, to make mistakes and to work outside the box, or they simply don't think – or care – about what they can and should do when faced with a challenging or unknown situation. Then, when things go bad, they typically make excuses instead of taking responsibility.

Whether from fear, uncertainty or apathy, most of the time, people are not proactive when it comes to preventing or solving problems, especially when it means trying something new or stepping outside the box. They wait for others to act first, or they ignore the situation and nothing is ever done. This inaction leads to customer problems or issues, or turns little problems into disasters.

I recently docked my boat at a maintenance yard and made them aware of two manufacturers' recalls that needed to be repaired over the summer. Shortly after, I sold the boat. I was dismayed to learn that when the new owner took the boat out, it didn't operate properly. Of course, he was upset and called me to complain. I called the maintenance crew to find out what happened, since the issue he complained about should have been repaired as one of the recalls and since their business had been reimbursed by the manufacturer for the work. I was told that the one repair was complete, but that when the boat sold, they stopped without calling or notifying either of us because they didn't know how to proceed. I asked why since I had authorized both repairs prior to the sale, the manufacturer had mandated they be fixed and they had been reimbursed for the work. At that point, they offered other excuses. They chose not to act because they didn't know what the change of ownership meant, yet they did not take the initiative to find out, either because of fear of repercussions that the work wasn't done, failure to think the situation through, or due to apathy. In the end, they fixed the boat, but lost two customers and damaged their reputation.

When people do take the initiative, when they listen to the customers' needs and proactively work to meet them, the outcome is very different.

Let's look at this case study.

I met a group of friends for a Sunday brunch buffet at one of our favorite restaurants. Unfortunately, one of the gang had to work and couldn't make it. I had an idea to box up some waffles and drop it off on our way home. I knew the policy didn't allow "to-go" boxes from the brunch, but hoped I could pay for an extra meal and take it to him. I presumed that my waitress wouldn't be comfortable bending the rules, so I asked her to get the hostess (who was also the manager), so I could talk with her. The waitress immediately found the manager. She didn't try to avoid involving her or "forget" to get her. She acted. The manager came over and I explained what I wanted to do, making sure to note that I intended to pay. She told me that the policy didn't allow "to-go" orders and then quickly added that she would tell our waitress to bring a box and leave it on the table. She said I should feel free to load up a plate with anything I wanted, but not to take the box to the buffet. She knew her primary job was to satisfy the customer, so she acted without hesitation or fear to do so, even if it meant stepping outside the box. I took a few waffles loaded with fixings and delivered it to my friend. Before leaving though, I left both the waitress and the manager a generous tip.

The manager exceeded our expectations. She knew that managing meant satisfying customers and acting as a role model for her people, so they could learn and succeed. She...

1. ...actively listened.

2. ...said yes instead of reverting to "policy."

3. ...found a creative solution.

4. ...modeled behavior to encourage her employee to think outside the box.

5. ...showed her employee that it's possible to communicate with and satisfy one customer without causing others to feel slighted.

6. ...created an environment for her employee that encouraged initiative and empowerment.

7. ...worked with her employee to ensure she succeeded, not only with that table, but in the future.

8. ...let her employee experience what success felt like – the employee was well-tipped.

By getting out of the box, the manager created a win-win-win scenario. The customer won because my need was met. The waitress (and manager) won because they received a generous tip. The business won by extending the loyalty of a group of regular customers, who undoubtedly will refer business.

This example also points out that often, the way a customer asks a question can dictate the response. This puts the burden of the relationship, the responsibility for finding a solution, on the customer, which is never where it should be. Think about the last time you were on an airplane and wanted a whole can of soda. If you ask for the can, the answer is generally, "No." If you take the cup and then ask for what's left in the can, you might get a "Yes."

Job	Meaningless	Meaningful
Dishwasher	Cleans dirty dishes used by other people.	Keeps people who will be using the dishes from getting sick.
Brick Layer	Builds a wall.	Builds a home or place for people to earn a living, so they can live with dignity.
Street Sweeper	Picks up others' trash.	Creates a beautiful neighborhood that people can be proud of, which may even help reduce crime.
School Custodian	Cleans up after kids and fixes things they break.	Creates a healthy, safe, positive learning environment.
Farm Laborer	Picks crops.	Feeds the community.

Job	Meaningless	Meaningful
Automotive Assembly Line Worker	Puts one part onto another like bolts onto an engine.	Builds transportation, so people can get to work, home, school and other places safely.
Seamstress	Makes clothes.	Helps people wear garments that keep them warm, boost their confidence and help them succeed.
Mortician	Works with dead bodies.	Provides respectful care and brings peace to families who lost loved ones.

The traits that stop people from acting in the best interest of the customer—fear, knowledge, apathy—may also be the result of how a person views their job and of their attitude about their job. It's about time that we all understand that every job has meaning. It's all in how you look at it, and how you look at it makes a huge impact on your attitude and commitment to performing it in the best possible way to delight the customer. Let's look at a few jobs from two different perspectives. First, we show a typical perspective, one in which the job is perceived as trivial or meaningless. Then, we look at it from a different, more positive point of view, one that gives meaning and value to each job. Try this exercise with jobs you consider trivial at your own company, and even with your own job. It might give you more respect for what you and others do. Every job has meaning and value. It's all in the way you look at it.

What does your job mean?

Knowing the ultimate meaning and value your job provides should motivate you to change your attitude from "I can't" to "I can," from making excuses to taking action and finding solutions, and from taking notes to actively listening. The person who listens before saying yes or no is always in the best position to take care of the customer. Listen first. Then make a decision on what you can and are willing to do, keeping in mind the value your job provides, parking your fear and discarding your apathy. And, don't be afraid to change your mind and your approach. Traditionally, changing your mind has always been seen as a weakness. But, in a world that's changing faster than ever, successful professionals realize that a genuine willingness to change their own minds is the ultimate advantage. It's a hallmark of someone who is focused on "I can." Look at what can happen when you take this approach.

- Jeff Bezos, the CEO of Amazon, launched Amazon Auctions, designed to compete with eBay. That didn't go as well as he wanted it to. So instead of sticking to his guns, he basically changed his mind and approach. He abandoned the old idea, pivoted and moved onto new ideas and that eventually became Amazon's highly profitable third-party sellers program. Bezos says, "Smart people constantly reconsider problems they thought they had solved. They are open to new points of view, new information and challenges to their own ways of thinking."

- Alan Mulally saved Ford Motor Company, not by staying the course, but by continually changing course in response to new data...to accommodate the unexpected delay [of introducing a new model, the Ford Edge], Mulally's overall plan for Ford would have to change. But that was the whole point. This mindset is the essence of agile leadership.

Finding solutions requires a commitment to taking action without apathy or fear. When this doesn't happen, tiny issues can become mountains or even disasters that are often covered up by "little white lies" or other excuses. These become difficult to remember and, eventually, they catch up with you, often in unexpected ways. And the longer it is from the time the lie was told or the excuse was given, the harder it is to recover with any credibility when caught. In fact, it often gets to the point where it's too late.

One of the companies we work with, an automobile dealership, has a policy that the salespeople always drive the car off the lot and into the community for about 15 minutes before turning the wheel over to the customer. This allows them to control the demo, point out features and continue to build a relationship with the customer. One salesperson, for some reason, found it difficult to explain to customers that this was standard company policy. Instead, he habitually told customers that it was an insurance requirement. Little did he know that on one test drive, the wife of the state attorney general was his customer. Curious, she asked her husband, who told her that there was no such rule. The attorney general went to the dealership and pointed out that the salesperson had lied and misrepresented facts to customers. The salesperson was promptly fired.

In another case, an employee was using a company car and backed into a pole. The employee immediately reported the accident per company policy. The first question the manager had was, "Are you ok?" The entire incident was given to the insurance company and completely taken care of. The employee was cautioned to be careful in the future, but greeted with relief that no one had been injured.

Why would anyone ever lie to avoid taking responsibility? The best thing to do is to tell the truth, to own up to your mistakes and offer solutions so they aren't repeated. Working from a place of fear or apathy makes this impossible.

The same is true when asked a question and you don't know the answer. If you don't know, tell the customer that you need to find out. Then do so and get back to the customer as soon as possible. Offer to find out immediately or to call the customer on their cell when you get the information. Give them the choice. This same fear and apathy that drives people to use little white lies prevents people from proactively making decisions to help customers. After all, if people break the rules to help the customer, they may have to admit it, which because of fear leads to the little white lie. It's a vicious cycle. Isn't it simpler to identify when you've made a mistake, own up to it and figure out how to fix it? The worst that you can imagine happening won't get any worse!

Think about it. What's the worst that can happen when you are honest, when you take responsibility? You may feel like you disappointed someone. You might lose a customer because they didn't get the answer they wanted (e.g. you are out of stock on a particular item or there is a delay in shipping your product). At the same time, people will trust you and admire your integrity. You will have an opportunity to find a solution that might prevent the same outcome next time.

Conversely, what's the worst that can happen when you tell a lie? Most likely, it will catch up with you and as a result, you will lose your job, people's trust and your integrity.

It is time to stop letting fear and apathy drive your behavior and replace it with confidence in your skills, your knowledge of what the customer wants and your ability to deliver it. Think about the enormous effort that goes into maintaining a lie. Wouldn't that effort have been better spent improving yourself and advancing your career?

Remember, your job is to help the customer. Which experience do you think any customer would want to have?

- Business A: The product is out of stock in the store. The person you are working with says, "I'm not really supposed to do this, but I want to help you out." You are taken into the back office and helped to use their computer to find the item and order it on the company's website. The person then gives you a choice of having the product shipped to the business (no delivery fee) for pick-up or to your home, and lets you know that you can return it to the business, if needed, instead of shipping it back. You place your order and are given a business card with instructions to call with any questions and go home.

- Business B: The product is out of stock. The person you are working with suggests you go home and check the Internet to see if you can find the product on their website and then order it for delivery. You ask if there is a way the person can help you order the product while you are in the business. You are told it's against policy and that the manager who can give permission is not in. You get a business card, which does not include the website and leave.

For whatever reason, when you don't follow this rule—"It's easier to ask forgiveness than permission"—everything grinds to a halt. It slows the sales process and frustrates, or worse, drives customers away. In taking time to track someone down who can give permission, you get so bogged down that you go beyond the close—you miss any opportunity of closing a sale or reconciling an issue. As a result, the business loses sales and growth slows. In addition, by not taking the initiative and doing whatever it takes to help the customer, managers get the impression that you lack initiative. Your performance declines and your advancement and raise are put on hold. You start to feel and be treated a bit like an outsider and the downward spiral continues.

This never has to happen. Instead of asking for permission, ask yourself with every customer interaction, "How do I gain the most value for my customer? How do I learn and take the opportunity to perform at a higher level?" Then, take the steps to make it happen. No excuses, only solutions.

In summary:

- Understand the value your job provides.
- Get rid of fear and apathy.
- Act with confidence and take the initiative.
- Ask forgiveness, not permission.
- Always take the longer-term view.
- Bring a solution to the table. Give the customer a choice.
- Tell the truth every time and don't make excuses—ever.
- If you know there is a mistake, own up to it.

It's All About You!

CHAPTER 8

They Never Forget

DID YOU EVER go to a store where you were mistreated, go somewhere else and get the royal treatment and buy their products, only to think about returning to the first store to show them what they missed? That's exactly what actress Julia Roberts did as Vivian Ward in the movie *Pretty Woman*. No one who has seen the movie could ever forget this famous line from perhaps the most memorable scene from the movie: "Big mistake! Big. Huge."

The line is delivered when Vivian Ward, loaded down with bags after having shelled out serious cash at another store, returns to an upscale boutique where condescending clerks had shunned her because she didn't look like she could belong.

By many standards, this is the best shopping montage of all time because, in that particular scene, Julia Roberts played the proverbial "everyman." Who has not felt like they've been shunned, disregarded, ignored, judged and made to feel inferior or unimportant as a customer? In this scene, Julia Roberts scored a win for all of us.

And like Julia Roberts' character, customers don't forget—ever—especially a bad experience. In fact, they amplify their feelings about the experience, a product, service and brand—at massive, revenue-impacting scale—by telling everyone they meet about it. And with the Internet, social media, blogs and texting, the number of people who hear about these bad experiences has grown exponentially.

How many people are you losing because you treat even one person poorly? What does providing bad service to one person cost your business when one complaint can go viral in minutes, whether or not the facts are accurate or embellished?

Think about the last time you were gathered at a party or a business convention telling stories. The bad stories always make for good tales and entertainment, not the good ones. Think about the last time you had a bad experience as a customer. How many people did you tell? Did you post it, tweet about it or otherwise share it online? In some extreme cases, people have made music videos that have gone viral, written blogs and even set up websites.

The Institute of Customer Service found that one in four social media users have used platforms to complain. Increasingly, platforms such as Twitter and Facebook are being viewed as the perfect vehicles for customers to escalate complaints, with 12% of the 2,195 consumers surveyed stating they had taken this course of action. The convenient and public nature of social media makes it an easy tool for shoppers to register their concerns. For example...

- Apparently arriving at the airport an hour and a half early isn't enough when the line to check in takes over an hour to get through. Thanks for nothing #americanairlines. Maybe rethink your queuing system to create some order. Three lines funneling into one teller just isn't working out for anyone. #badservice

- Stopped at the 7-11 on 522 where I always get my coffee and gas... I wanted to use my Belly rewards points I earned (on eight other purchases there) to pay for my coffee, the manager said ok, took my points from my card, then refused to give me the coffee free, since he won't honor the belly rewards program, only the 7-11 app... then why offer it or even take my points off? I put my other items back and paid for my FREE coffee, since I had already taken a drink. Can't believe he lost a regular customer who comes in every day over $1.81...#badservice #7eleven

Social media has the power to take one "shared" negative experience and communicate it to thousands–even millions–of people.

Now the bad news–for every one customer who complains, at least 25 remain silent but take action in other ways that negatively impact a business. Studies have shown that 53% of customers altered their buying habits for one or more years after having a bad experience. Losing even a single customer can be very costly. It's critical for companies to turn a complaint into a positive for the customer and for the company.

How much is poor service costing you?

On the other hand, what happens when customers receive exceptional service or what we call the Red Carpet Treatment? While some customers will share their positive experiences, news of bad customer service still reaches more than twice as many ears as praise for a good service experience. Why? It is simple. People expect to receive good customer service every time and everywhere they go. It's the expectation, the norm, not the exception.

What's at the heart of good or bad service? You are. It is up to you to ensure that every customer is taken care of, to delight them so much so that they are one of the few who do share positive stories and recommend your business. It's up to you to make every customer feel like they are the center of attention, the most important VIP your business ever had. That's the Red Carpet Treatment.

Businesses often are organized primarily around selling products rather than creating customers. They talk about *customer* value instead of *customized* value. They fail to understand the difference between the two. Customer value is about delivering generic value to a potential customer. Customized value is about selecting and delivering a solution for each customer. To customize value, a salesperson must always:

1. Offer real help and show a genuine interest in their needs. Courtesy and friendliness aren't enough.

2. Provide help selecting the right product or service for their individual needs, wants and desires.

3. Ask questions that are direct, but non-confrontational or pushy and deliver specific information that builds on moving the process forward.

4. Find out exactly what the needs, wants and desires are of the customer. When they seek financial advice, they want peace of mind. When they get an eye exam, they want to see better. When they look for clothes, they want to look good and be comfortable.

5. Offer to show the customer how the product or service works for them, and then let them experience it for themselves.

It's not enough to "connect the dots" between customer needs and your company's offering. You must also connect with the individuals who will be affected by your offering, and help them understand how buying from you will satisfy their needs, wants and desires. When you do this, you are helping customers select the product that is right for each of them.

You are involving them, interacting with them and providing a quality selection, not simply working to close a sale. With this approach, price–the primary roadblock to closing most sales–becomes a distant consideration.

Unfortunately, without consistent training on customer-centric selling, nearly all salespeople revert to the standard, *"Hi. Can I help you?"* This enables customers to pre-qualify themselves before learning about the products. *"No. I'm just looking. Thanks."* This forces the salesperson to make a judgment about the customer's true intent without getting to know them. *("They are window shopping and not really buyers.")*

For every one customer who complains, at least 25 remain silent but take action in other ways that negativily impact a business

Customers want the Red Carpet Treatment, to be appreciated and to feel special. One accounting firm I know of was meeting a client on his birthday. The client was discussing business with the CPA when the staff walked in with a small birthday cake singing, "Happy Birthday." The look on his face was unforgettable. There is no doubt that this client will remember the surprise for a long time and tell others – potential clients – about it.

In another case, a colleague told me he was meeting his family for lunch at a local diner. As they entered, the hostess greeted them warmly by name and found them a quiet table. Despite being busy, the entire staff made them feel important and special. While dining, his daughter was telling her mom about the necklace she had on. She had bought it from a little shop in a nearby town that she always goes to. She explained that they know her by name, call her if they are going to have a sale and give her a goodwill discount on everything she buys, just to say, "Thank you."

These little things make a huge impact. Ensuring clients feel appreciated reinforces their decision to work with you. Going the extra step to communicate your commitment to them, to give them that reassurance that they're in the right place, makes a huge difference. It's the little unexpected touches, like birthday cakes or goodwill discounts that get that message across. Those touches keep clients happy and your business growing.

The Red Carpet Treatment doesn't have to be expensive, time consuming or onerous. It just needs to be thoughtful. And, giving your clients the Red Carpet Treatment is the best business decision you will ever make.

So here's my question for you: what are you going to do today to show genuine appreciation to the people who have chosen to do business with you and to those who have not yet decided? This is no 'one size fits all' – you need to think about what would mean the most to them. And it's not just your clients that need appreciation. It's the people who refer you, your business neighbors and of course, the most important people in your business – your employees. They all need the Red Carpet Treatment.

Red Carpet Treatment is not a luxury in business today. It's a necessity if you want to stand out from the crowd, prove differentiation and sell on quality of service, not on price.

And remember – when customers don't get the Red Carpet Treatment, they never forget.

It's All About You!

CHAPTER 9

Help Me Understand

I DON'T' UNDERSTAND.

Why do businesses spend enormous sums of money to stay on the cutting edge of technology, marketing and systems, but then make it virtually impossible to do work with them?

This happens across industries, in business-to-consumer and business-to-business situations, every day. In fact, at some time or another, it happens in virtually every business. Take, for example, a car dealership we know in the Boston area. They continuously spend money to update their facilities with state-of-the-art equipment, from computers and software, to the solar panels on the roof. This commitment has become part of their public image. Even with all these "bells and whistles," it is well known in the community that it is very difficult to buy from them. A friend of mine, who was looking for a new truck, told me that he was planning to buy from this establishment. Knowing their reputation and having had personal experience, I told my friend what he might expect.

My friend went anyway. He arrived, parked, looked at some of the trucks on the lot and found one he wanted to drive, but no one was around to help him. While standing next to the truck, he used his cell phone to call the dealership. Before talking to anyone, a recording informed him that his "call may be monitored for quality and training purposes." When he reached the receptionist, he asked her to send out a salesperson to help him. The receptionist told him, "We don't do that here. You have to come into the showroom." And then, she hung up. He called back and again asked the receptionist politely to please send someone out, so he didn't have to walk all the way to the building and back. She hung up. He called back again, but this time, he told her what he thought about their service and business, got in his truck and drove off to a different dealership where he bought a truck. Despite the fact that this dealership had exceptional products, facilities, location, technology and marketing, they made it extremely difficult to buy a vehicle from them, even when fully intending to.

I don't understand. Why any business would employ someone as the customers' first point of contact who won't do their job and find someone to help the customer? Or, why they would put people in place without training and educating them on how best to do their jobs? This business has the technology to monitor calls for training purposes, but it doesn't use what it learns to improve quality and performance. The people they employ consistently treat customers with indifference, and like with the receptionist, poor service is the norm.

Why do businesses invest tens of thousands of dollars to get ahead in every aspect of technology–their infrastructure and business systems, their website, Internet marketing, CRM systems, email and social media marketing–to drive traffic into their stores, but fail to invest in training and educating their people on how to take care of customers? If a company's professionals can't provide the Red Carpet Treatment–or any help at all–what is the point of spending money on technology and marketing? Technology doesn't sell products and services. People do.

> *Salespeople and management need to adopt the attitude that tells customers, "We do business your way."*

Part of the problem is that, in most cases, businesses measure customer satisfaction only after people buy, so they have no idea how many customers they actually lose. The number one complaint among customers is having to wait, or that trying to purchase something – a car, a dress, groceries or services – takes too long. This underscores the fact that the majority of customers are lost long before they have the opportunity to actually buy, not because they couldn't find the right product or service. Without an accurate customer count – a count of every person who enters or contacts a business – management will never know how many potential customers they had and how many were lost because no one would help them. Most salespeople are not interested in listening to the customer to find out their needs, wants and desires in a product or service. Essentially, they tell customers, "This is how we work. These are the products or services we want to push today. Do it our way or leave." Salespeople – and management – need to learn to work from the customer's perspective. They should adopt the attitude that tells customers, "We do business *your* way."

Opportunities for sales present themselves every single day. Every person who comes to or contacts a business represents an opportunity for a sale. These customers come to the business seeking expert guidance and help to first find the right product or service – one that matches their needs, wants and desires – and second, to purchase it at the right price. No opportunity will ever come to fruition if a business doesn't have people who are interested in and trained to work with and help customers buy cars.

It is time that all businesses and the people working there start focusing on customers. It is time that you start putting customers first. After all, customers don't just wander in randomly. They do their research and make a concerted effort to come to a business. They stand in front of a salesperson ready to buy. While technology may help bring customers in, it's the people that keep them and turn them into customers.

I don't understand why businesses insist on investing in enormous sums of money in technology, infrastructure and systems, and not in their people.

———

"When you take care of customers, they will become loyal clients."

———

SECTION 2

Customers Have The Power

It's All About You!

"Care."

It's All About You!

CHAPTER 10

Avoiding Culture Shock

EVERY BUSINESS EXISTS because of you. You are the customer. It's a business's job to meet your needs, to solve problems and meet demands. Customers must always come first. After all, without customers, there is no business.

In essence, customers have the power. Who knew?

As the customer, you drive profits, pay employees and provide resources for the business to use as an investment to fuel growth. When this happens, the business becomes a customer as well.

Customers expect everyone in your business to care about their needs and to help them find the right product or service to satisfy them. When this happens every day with every customer, a business thrives; it has a customer-centric environment. To continue thriving, a business must continue this effort; it can never stop. It should move forward and continually elevate the customer experience and nurture customer relationships.

Without this type of environment, customers often experience a type of culture shock, a disconnect, between their expectations and reality. It's the shock that comes from realizing that a business is more intent on profits than on customers. It's the shock that comes when it's clear that the person hired to help you could not care less about you, the job or the business. And it's the last thing any customer should ever experience. Yet surprisingly, it's more common than most think.

A woman went to her bank – Bank of America – to cash some savings bonds for her son. She asked what the process was. The teller told her they did not cash savings bonds, even though the woman knew that any financial institution or bank in the United States has the ability and authority to do so. The woman politely started to explain that she had checked first, and then tried to ask a question when the teller interrupted her. She quietly asked the teller to let her finish her question at which point the teller loudly chastised the woman saying, "Step back in line. I am not going to help you." The woman was literally shocked, speechless and embarrassed, not only in front of her son, but in front of a long line of customers at the bank, some of whom she knew. Keeping her cool, the woman calmly asked to speak to a manager. The teller made a face and then reluctantly went to find a manager. As they walked back to the counter, the teller was talking to the manager the entire time and pointing at the woman. The manager asked what the problem was and the woman told him what had happened. She explained that if Bank of America did not cash savings bonds, it was no problem, but she was trying to understand the situation, which is why she was trying to ask a question. The woman actually knew more about how to cash savings bonds than the teller, it turns out, because the manager said all that was needed was a valid driver's license. Behind the manager, the teller kept rolling her eyes, sneering, shaking her head and mouthing denials the entire time the manager and the woman were talking.

At this point, the woman told the manager that she did not want to work with that teller since she was impolite. The manager said okay, but told her she'd have to go to the back of the line. At that point, the woman asked the manager if he was serious, what happened to customer service and did all customers have to wait in line so long only to be mistreated and embarrassed. Only then did the manager direct her to a teller who was not helping anyone else, so that she could get help.

The teller, and to some extent the manager, used every one of the words that should never ever be used with a customer–No, Don't, Can't and Won't. She told the woman **no**, they **don't** cash savings bonds and she **can't** help. She then even went so far as to say, "I **won't** help you." The customer was polite; the teller was rude. In this situation, the customer exercised tremendous restraint; not everyone would continue to be pleasant. The situation could easily have escalated, and then no one would have been satisfied.

This is an example of culture shock in the extreme. The customer expected to be treated with respect, but received the opposite. Without a doubt, this bank failed to build a customer-centric environment and culture.

It's the exact opposite of how TD Bank treats its customers. At this bank, customers are called by name and thanked on arrival. "Thank you for banking with us, Mr. Libin. How can I help you today?" If you arrive 10 to 15 minutes early, they open the doors instead of making you wait. If they close at six and you are still in line, they stay open just a little longer to ensure every customer is served. They go out of their way to be exceptionally nice, provide exceptional service and to keep your business.

In a customer focused culture, regardless of the business, every process starts and ends with customer satisfaction in mind. When a customer walks in the door, everything else should stop. Customers should be the focus of everyone's attention, not in a manner that makes them feel uncomfortable, but in a way that ensures they receive the information and assistance they need when they need it. As a result, a business will achieve increased customer loyalty and financial gain.

So, how does a business accomplish this?

First, the customer must be the heart of a business. If not, you don't have a business. Everything must be about the customer, delivering exceptional service and a positive experience. Achieving a high satisfaction rating only tells you about those who purchased. What about the ones who walked away without buying? How do you measure that?

Exceptional service and customer relationships must be core values of the organization and every person who works for it, beginning with the owners and/or management. While this might seem to be obvious, clearly articulating it and modeling customer-centric behavior and principles has a deep impact on the business, from strategy and attitude toward customers, to how each employee sees their role in meeting the needs of customers. This will help lay the foundation for a customer-centric culture.

Second, be sure every employee is aware of the company's commitment to customers as a core value.

It's critical that the values are not simply words, but words that translate to attitude and action. Unless the majority of the organization embraces a customer-centric environment, it will never become a reality.

Be aggressive in communicating the impact of customer satisfaction on the company's performance. Make sure that employees and anyone associated with your company knows that customer satisfaction is a core business value. Visibly communicate this core value using posters, pictures, banners and other signs. In short, make it clear to anyone who enters your business that customer satisfaction is a top priority. Show employees how they benefit directly from long-term financial gains, increased brand image and growth in customer loyalty.

Involve everyone with customers. Most businesses have customer service departments, customer service representatives or others whose sole responsibility is customer service, yet everyone's business is customer service. It's not enough to expect these people to do it all. Building a customer-centric culture is everyone's responsibility, including product development and design teams, sales and services departments, and key decision makers. For example, the CEO of Groove consistently spends 20 or more hours each week sitting with his support teams, listening, interacting and learning from customers. This is critical. When management and owners model customer-centric behavior, other employees will learn and adopt their behavior.

Third, put customer satisfaction ahead of everything else. Period.

Simply stating that customer service is important is not enough. It has to be more than a simple statement or motto. It has to be real and put into action. Everything must revolve around the customer. According to the *Harvard Business Review*, research demonstrates that when customers contact companies for service, they care most about two things: Is the frontline employee knowledgeable? And, is the problem resolved on the first call? More than half of the customers surveyed across industries say they've had a bad service experience. Nearly the same fraction think many of the companies they interact with don't understand or care about them. On average, 40% of customers who suffer through bad experiences stop doing business with the offending company. By putting customers first, above all else, you are putting your most important stakeholder first. Beyond the obvious, this includes making sacrifices and doing whatever you have to do to make things right. Keeping in line with the organization's core values, a company's people must be confident that they will be appreciated for foregoing other tasks and giving up personal time for ensuring customer satisfaction. Remember, customers pay salaries and drive profits.

Putting customer satisfaction first also means that employees must be empowered to act in the best interest of the customer and make decisions. It's as if they are mini-managers. If the manager can fix it, why can't employees? Why don't they have the same power to the make decisions that will make the experience better for consumers? People need to have the authority to make the on-the-spot decisions that are right for the customer. Give your people ownership to take care of the problem. And fix it. Encourage them to make decisions when required. In addition, organizations must deliver exceptional service that goes beyond the sale. They care about the value and experience they deliver to the customer. They are committed to following up, keeping in touch and helping to resolve issues that may arise in the relationship.

Fourth, hire the right people. Educate and train people to execute at a level consistent with your way of thinking. Realize that at some time or another, everyone makes a bad pick. When you do, and the wrong individual was hired, make a decision quickly. Don't linger with a problem that could become a long-term illness. Move on. As a manager, you must make a decision and move on.

Doing business in a way that puts customers at the heart of an organization includes hiring the right people, communicating that customer centricity is a core value of your company and clearly setting expectations. On a side note, I've used the term customer-centric to this point as most people generally understand the term. And while some businesses use this term to describe their commitment, I call it doing business in the best way possible. Every new hire must understand the value placed on taking care of the customer. They need to understand that they play a vital role in maintaining customer relationships. They must be willing and able to take the extra step for their customers. This is an important point. They must have the ability to deliver exceptional service. This requires ongoing education and training.

Management must evaluate, coach and help their people reach their goals. It's a manager's job to help their people succeed. If companies don't provide the resources and tools that allow people to succeed in this effort, the values will never become reality in practice. Finally, when all else fails, creating customer relationships may mean changing people's jobs or, in some cases, helping them move on so they can find the right industry or job. In their current role, they may be misemployed. In the long run, the business will be better off without those who don't commit to the company's core values.

Building long-term customer relationships goes beyond people. It should be evident in the company's process and even in the design and layout of a retail location or website.

Why do Costco and Wal-Mart have greeters? These greeters are placed at the door to make customers feel welcome and to offer assistance from the moment a customer enters the store. It's the store's first opportunity to show shoppers that they are customer-friendly establishment and committed to making every experience a positive one.

Think about the approach used by Apple Stores. There is always someone at the door who can help direct you to your destination, which is usually another person further in the store or the Genius Bar. All the newest, "hottest" items are at the front of the store while accessories and smaller items are in the back. This system draws customers into the store, so they have the opportunity to look at, touch and experience virtually any device Apple sells. Apple also makes it convenient to get service by allowing customers to schedule appointments in advance, or when they arrive, so that they know waiting will be minimized. Finally, they offer free classes, typically before store hours, which provide 1-1 support after the sale and opens opportunities for additional purchases.

> *Every process should start and end with customer satisfaction in mind. Everything should focus on the end result.*

Supermarkets are strategically set up to make it easy for customers to shop and, at the same time, to encourage them to walk from one end of the store to the other. Placing the produce, dairy, meat and frozen foods in different areas of the store is a strategic decision. End caps are reserved for "special promotions," which are paid for by manufacturers.

Everything and everyone should align with the company's values and make it easy for customers to do business with your organization.

Fifth, reward employees and celebrate successes.

Employees at every level and in every job should be recognized for delivering exceptional customer service, resolving issues and for finding new ways to build and expand a customer-centric culture. This means aligning every part of the business with the sole purpose of creating an optimal experience for customers every time they interact with your company. For this to become a reality, you need a motivated team that understands their personal gains – promotions, bonuses, salary increases and more – are tied to customer centricity.

Nordstrom, the upscale department store, built their business and their success on excellent customer service. And they are a near perfect example of a company that follows these five steps.

The company was started more than a century ago in 1901 by John W. Nordstrom and Carl F. Wallin as a shoe retailer in Seattle, Washington. For years, every employee at Nordstrom's was given a copy of the employee handbook, a single index card with 75 words. That card today has just one rule, "Use good judgment in all situations."

Nordstrom works hard to hire personable, capable people whose judgment can be relied on to represent the company. They create an environment that supports these employees with generous salaries, a pleasant work environment and good working conditions. They consistently appear on *Fortune*'s "Best Companies to Work For" Top 100, ranking around 50th.

Employee empowerment, the ability to "use your best judgment" is imperative to delivering Nordstrom-quality customer service. In one case, a customer's shoes were delivered to her home and left outside by Federal Express in the rain. The package and shoes were soaked and ruined. While FedEx was responsible, the customer called Nordstrom. The salesperson never once suggested filing a claim with FedEx. She immediately said, "I'm so incredibly sorry that happened and I'm bringing over a brand new pair of shoes. Will you be home in forty-five minutes?"

Nordstrom's goal is to provide excellent customer service, so people not only buy more at one time, but always come back for more. For this, a set of internal standards is set, like the no-questions-asked return policy. While it is true that Nordstrom's customer service handbook is a one-liner, other methods, notably hiring exceptionally capable people, training and modeling the expected standards, giving them the authority to make decisions and rewarding them accordingly, all contribute to their "putting the customer first" business model.

Building a business that focuses on the customer has long-term financial and business benefits. Starting with your core values and extending through rewarding success, the time and attention spent on customer relationships will be well worth it in the long run.

*"There is only one
NOW that counts."*

It's All About You!

CHAPTER 11

Work on Customer Timeframe

WORK ON THE customer's timeframe. We've all experienced the high-pressure sale, the push to "buy now" before it's too late! While many salespeople believe this approach works, stories abound of customers who simply walked away because they didn't like the pressure.

Does it really make a difference whether customers buy now, or if they come back when they are truly ready? If you keep pushing customers to buy now, you will run them off.

In fact, traditional sales methods have always focused on closing the sale, NOW. As a result, many customers feel pressured and uncomfortable with the salesperson, and by default, with the business or store, and they leave. Buyers become shoppers and the business loses opportunities to create long-term clientele who will return time and again. The question becomes, "Is your business or store seeking to do business or simply to do business NOW?" What is the goal? The answer should be, "To build clientele that will return and shop repeatedly, not simply to close a quick sale NOW, today, right this moment."

If you don't give the customer time to do their homework, to consider their options and to get all the information they need to make an intelligent decision, it won't help you close the deal. The customer can't make the decision because something is missing.

Look at it this way. A roofer shows up at your house and asks how soon you will be replacing your roof. Unless there is a leak or major damage, you can't answer that question properly. You don't have key information like how much will it cost, how critical is it to replace it now, does the whole roof need replacing or only a portion and why should you hire this particular roofer.

A serious misconception in the sales world is that business must be transacted immediately – NOW. As a result, sales professionals – many of whom really know better – repel customers or end up persuading customers to purchase something that doesn't meet their needs that they can't afford, that they really don't want or that leaves them dissatisfied after making the purchase. While this seems to indicate that high pressure selling works, in reality, it leads customers who feel they were coerced into making a purchase to permanently avoid the business in the future, to tell everyone they know about their bad experience and to post negative reviews on social media, in the long run causing more harm than good.

No matter how hard the push is to buy NOW, the result is usually the same: if it is not the right product for the customer, nothing will make them buy, not even price. If customers are planning to buy, they will, when they are ready, with or without you. They'll make a purchase when they've been given enough time to consider their options and enough information to determine the best choice. Pressuring them by saying that promotions will end, prices may rise or the supply will run out, doesn't speed up the process. In fact, these high-pressure techniques may actually drive customers away and send them down the road to your competition. Keep in mind that if a client doesn't do business with you NOW, it doesn't mean he won't do business with you later, if you respect their need to make a decision on their timeline, not yours. The bottom line is that if you don't know what you are getting into, you won't spend the money.

In the sales world, there is only one true definition of NOW. It's when the customer is ready to buy and take the product home. Salespeople who understand this steer away from the hard-sell approach and embrace a low-pressure consultative process that results in a more positive experience for the customer and longer-term gains for the business. Salespeople who adopt this approach don't sell customers on a product or service. They help them buy the right product or service. They work with customers to learn about their needs.

They ask a wide range of probing questions and actively listen. They are 100% present throughout the process.

Think about your last visit to your doctor, perhaps when you had a cold or flu. As well as giving you a physical examination, your doctor most likely asked you whether you had been experiencing fevers, chills, a sore throat and perhaps body aches. The doctor probably asked a multitude of questions and only then reached a diagnosis and prescribed medication. As a patient, you feel like the doctor takes the time to listen to you and cares about your well-being. It's this feeling that earns your trust and keeps you coming back to this physician. The cost of the visit and treatment are never a factor in who you choose to see.

This is very much like the low-pressure consultative sales approach, except instead of a diagnosis or a prescription, you are finding the most suitable products and services for your customer.

The question becomes: Is your business looking to do business or simply looking to do business NOW? When a customer walks in, the goal should be to develop, gain and then retain their business. Whether they buy today or NOW, next week or next month, doesn't matter. What matters is that they buy, that they buy from you and that they do so repeatedly.

Before this happens, you have to give them a reason to buy. For example, you may tell an office manager that replacing computers at the business every three years—the length of the typical warranty—is a smart strategy. Then, tell the customer that it is a smart strategy because in that period of time, parts and components will have reached their life span and will start to wear out or fail. Technology will have advanced significantly and new computers will perform even more functions, faster than ever. Prices will have come down, so the investment in replacing them will far outweigh the repairs they are sure to start needing. It's your job to be sure customers have enough information to make intelligent decisions. Doing this requires a game plan that should be followed each and every time with each and every customer.

1. Listen to customers' needs, wants and desires.

2. Help them select the product or service that meets their criteria.

3. Let them experience the product or service; let them try it on or see a demonstration.

4. Give them a reason to buy. Help them understand why they need it or would want to have it.

5. Only at the end, talk about price.

In the sales world, there is only one true definition of NOW. It's when the customer is ready to buy and take the product home.

It's All About You!

CHAPTER 12

If You Don't Love It Here, Leave

BUILDING LONG-TERM CUSTOMER relationships requires you to establish an emotional connection. Caring about customer service—not just satisfying customers, but going the extra mile—is not enough. The relationship is what keeps customers coming back over and over again. Building and maintaining customer relationships takes commitment and hard work. It takes people who are interested in caring about customers, not just sales. It's a hard job, talking to customers hour after hour every day. Not everyone can do it. So how do you know you are the right person?

At online shoe retailer Zappos, they pay people to quit. After an immersive training program on the company's strategy, culture and commitment to customers, every new hire is given "The Offer." They say to their newest employees, "If you quit today, we will pay you for the amount of time you've worked, plus we will offer you a $1,000 bonus." Why? Because if you're willing to take the company up on The Offer, you obviously don't have the sense of commitment they are looking for.

The point is that achieving customer service requires people who are fully committed, passionate, determined and devoted to making every experience for the customer positive. These people bring a positive attitude to work every day. You never hear them whine, "Oh, it's Monday, I have to go to work." They love their jobs.

The most important professional decision we make every day is the attitude we choose to express when dealing with customers. This vital choice can determine our success or failure in any job. It can build or strengthen relationships with customers or send them running to your competition. It's your choice. You purposefully choose your attitude for the day, for the hour, for the moment. You can decide to react angrily to a driver who cuts you off, or to be thankful you avoided an accident and hope that they get to their destination safely. While embracing a positive attitude can lead to virtually unlimited success, a negative attitude will lead to unhappiness, poor relationships, difficulty at work and ultimately, failure.

Where does attitude come from? This is a very powerful question. Most often, the answer is from somewhere or someone else; it's never your fault. People say work, people, traffic or something else like a slow or malfunctioning computer system caused it. Wrong. Attitude comes from within, from your thoughts, your mindset and your actions. You determine your attitude. While the tendency is to blame others, circumstances or events, how you respond to those things or people is governed by your attitude, not by what is happening.

Pause for a moment and think about your day. Was there ever a time where you felt frustrated or angry? What happened to trigger this? How did you choose to react? If you'd had a positive attitude, would your reaction and actions been different? Remember, you choose to respond in a positive or negative way. Think about the woman in the bank who was trying to cash her savings bonds. She remained calm and kept a positive attitude throughout the entire incident, unlike the teller who had a negative attitude from the start. Each of these individuals made a conscious choice in that instant about their attitude – positive or negative – and about how they would react and act. What is your attitude?

You may be thinking, "I don't have a bad attitude. I just look at things realistically." This is exactly what it sounds like – an excuse for being negative. Salespeople with negative attitudes struggle and have difficulty closing sales. Evidence of a negative or poor attitude at work includes laziness, tardiness, rudeness, rumor-mongering or any other activity that lowers overall morale. All these lead to decreased performance, not only for the one employee, but for others. Negative attitudes can spread and have a huge impact on the business. Negative people will search out others and attempt to bring them down to their level. This is how negative attitudes spread. Their negative influence feels powerful and they use it as a self-esteem boost. People do this in an attempt to feel better about themselves, but the end result is short-lived and unproductive. If your customers encounter bad attitudes from your employees, they won't come back. Customers don't want to deal with rude or apathetic employees.

Life – and work – is what you make it. Choose to make it positive. If you don't, you may not be the right person for the job you have now.

People like to be around positive people. In business, customers like to buy from positive people who have confidence in what they are selling and help their customers who enjoy the buying process. People do not want to be sold, but they love to buy. Having a positive attitude will improve your customer relationships and lead to success. Maintaining a positive attitude can be difficult, especially when things don't turn out the way you hoped and planned. If you look at every experience as an opportunity to learn, it's easier to keep a positive attitude. Face the facts in a positive light and move on. Become stronger from the experience, rather than weaker. Learn from your experiences and choose a positive attitude that prepares you for the next challenge, which usually is right around the corner.

Over the years, I've come to believe that there are basically two types of people – those who take responsibility for their lives and those who blame others and believer that it's always somebody else's fault. People who take responsibility are positive and proactive. They see the world as a wonderful, exciting place. They are the doers. They make a conscious decision to be this way every moment of their lives. Which one are you?

Zappos had a good point. Sometimes, people are simply misemployed. The job is not the right fit. If this is the case, even though it's a difficult and uncomfortable decision, when it's the right choice, it will be better in the long run for you and your company to move on. Often, people don't realize that they are unhappy in their job until someone points it out to them. When that happens, some people will try to improve the situation, others embrace a negative attitude and complain about it and others go into denial believing that the situation isn't as bad as they think.

If the following apply to you, it's quite possible that you are misemployed.

- You lack passion.
- You dislike the people you work with.
- You don't fit in with the corporate culture.
- You don't believe in the company.
- Your work performance is suffering.
- Your skills are not being utilized.
- Your input is not being heard or taken.
- You're bored or stagnating.
- You're consistently stressed.
- You're negative.
- You're unhappy.

If you can say yes to five or more of these, you are probably misemployed. If only a few apply, or if they apply at different times, check your attitude. Many of these may be fixed by adopting a new attitude. If not, moving on may be the best choice. If you don't love it, leave it.

Your attitude affects everyone around you. It affects your home life, your colleagues and even your customers. Would you rather go to a business and deal with a person with a bad attitude or a good attitude?

Airlines are a great example of this. Flying is a hassle for most people that is exacerbated by people around you with bad attitudes – the gate agent, the TSA agents, flight attendants and fellow passengers. Even if you leave late and arrive on time, when asked, "How was the flight?" most respond, "Not great." All you remember is the people. The flight could have been perfect, but all that you remember is the people you encountered along the way. It makes you wonder why these people work for the airlines or airports.

Your Job - *you have a choice*

At Southwest, you know the answer to this question. They fly for fun! They fly because they enjoy their jobs and each other and they feel appreciated by management, their coworkers and their passengers. Sure, they have great prices for the most part, but so do other airlines. It's not always about price. The culture at Southwest is to have fun and to be sure everyone around you does, too, including passengers. Even their ads and commercials exemplify the pervasiveness of this culture as they involve everyone – flight attendants, baggage handlers, ticket agents and more. They know that every person at Southwest has an important job, and they understand that it's more than the typical perception. Baggage handlers make sure clothes, gifts and other items arrive on the same plane and in good condition; flight attendants keep passengers safe and save lives in emergencies; pilots safely transport hundreds of people and families to their destination; and ticket agents inform, educate and deal with crises. If you truly think about the impact your job has on others, it will change your perception and attitude.

Resolve now to think deeply about your job and the far reaching impact it has on others. Then, bring a positive attitude to every facet of what you do. Have fun with people, so they remember that you made them smile and laugh and feel good while working with them. Build a relationship.

Exceed their expectations.

I was at the post office and one of the clerks stepped in to help me with a lost package. The customer at the next window turned to me and said, "Now you're in good hands. Frank will take great care of you!" Several people behind me echoed his remarks and Frank thanked them each by name. Everyone wants to work with a "Frank" wherever they go to transact business.

Think about your mindset. If you don't want to go to work, don't. If you get up feeling like it's going to be a bad day, it will be. If you expect to have a good day, it will happen. You will never disappoint yourself.

It's your choice. You can choose to be the "Frank" of your business.

It's All About You!

CHAPTER 13

Do You Want Customers or Clients?

WHILE THE WORDS customer and client are often used interchangeably, there is a clear distinction in their meaning. According to the *American Heritage Dictionary*, a customer is a person who buys goods or services from a store or business, and a client is someone who also receives professional services. It's all about the relationship. Customers are typically those who come to your business for a specific product or service. They come in, make a purchase with very little interaction and leave. Customers can be one-time or repeat patrons, but lack loyalty to the salesperson (you), the products or services or the company that provides them. They often shop around for the best deal. On the other hand, clients, in addition to buying your products or services, come to you seeking advice and solutions personalized to their particular needs, wants and desires. They trust you, the solutions you offer and the company you work for. They have a relationship with you, one that you have nurtured carefully, thoughtfully and sincerely.

Unfortunately, businesses, such as retail stores, restaurants, service stations, supermarkets, banks and home products stores, typically consider their patrons as customers. In doing so, they miss a tremendous opportunity to nurture and build loyal clientele, or even worse, they miss the opportunity to appreciate and keep those who already are loyal clients. Businesses of all types can establish closer relationships and turn customers into clients. It you are not convinced, answer these five questions as quickly as you can:

1. Where do you shop for groceries?

2. What is the brand of your mobile phone?

3. What's the name of your bank?

4. Where do you tell friends to go to get a good steak?

5. What brand of computer do you use?

Now, think about your answers. Are these the businesses you patronize first and most often? Chances are you answered yes to at least one question. If so, you are not simply their customer, you are their client.

Why are clients preferred over customers?

Clients are committed to doing business with a particular business and to patronizing that business repeatedly. Clients recommend the products and services offered by that business to friends and other associates. Clients buy the same brand for an extensive period of time.

While the benefits of building clientele are evident for businesses, there are also benefits for clients. Maintaining a solid relationship with a business reduces the client's perceived risk and cultivates their confidence in the products and services, the business and the professionals who work there. Clients make decisions more easily and with less stress because they begin to purchase or frequent a business out of habit rather than having to make repeated, conscious decisions. By building relationships, salespeople have a better understanding of their clients' needs. This reduces the time and effort patrons spend supplying new information and communicating problems or product needs.

Satisfied customers can go anywhere but loyal clients will always come back to you.

Remember, satisfied customers can go anywhere, but only loyal clients want to come to you. Turning a client into a devoted advocate is indispensable.

Building loyalty and developing client relationships is a long-term investment. It requires care, patience and a good plan. It requires consistently high quality work, the ability to listen, learn and anticipate client needs and dedication to building trust and respect. A loyal client can be your best and most important advocate.

It's All About You!

CHAPTER 14

Reach Up and Beyond

A BUSINESS IS only as good as the clients it serves – and keeps. Loyal clients and their repeat purchases are the cornerstones of long-term business success. For most businesses, it costs between four and 10 times more to acquire a new customer than it does to keep an existing one. In some cases, the cost of acquiring a new customer is over 30 times that of keeping an existing one. Once a prospective customer becomes a buyer, it's important not to overlook or ignore their needs as repeat customers become clients and are the foundation on which profitable businesses are built.

Unfortunately, many salespeople view their jobs as one transaction after another. They sell something and move on to the next sale. That's where they stop. They erroneously think they are in the business of selling things – automotive parts, home remodeling or repairs, printing services, financial consulting, tutoring or signs. In reality, they are all in the people business. They are not selling things; they are helping people select the right "thing" for their needs, wants and desires. Learning how to make people feel important and cared about is a critical skill, not only for the immediate sale, but for building long-term client relationships that lead to referrals and more important, to repeat business, year after year.

Some of the best examples of building relationships can be found in the restaurant business. Patrons know the names of the owners, hosts and servers, and vice versa. Beyond their names, many restaurant workers know something about their loyal clientele as well. They know if their guests prefer coffee or tea with breakfast. They may even remember their favorite meal or "the usual."

> ## It's not how much you know. It's how much you care.

If you received that class of service and if your favorites are automatically served to you without having to ask or explain your preferences, how would it make you feel? It would make me feel at home, or as if I was at the home of a good friend, someone who knows me well and wants me to have what I want. This type of relationship is ideal when it comes to serving your clients' needs in any industry or market, and it can be developed and nurtured regardless of the product or service you sell.

In addition to making sure that every client receives the best care during the purchase process, it is imperative to deliver the same high caliber of experience after the sale. People like to do business with people who care about them and who take an interest that goes beyond making a sale. During the initial sale, talk to your clients, listen to their answers and take notes. Keep potentially important information on hand like birthdays, marital status, children's names and ages, whether or not they have pets, their hobbies and how they spend their leisure time.

When you make people feel important even after the sale, they come to rely on your business and on you, and they trust you to have their needs and interests at heart. The following action plan will help you get started.

1. There's no such thing as over-communicating, as long as you are adding value and respecting their time and preferences. Clients depend on you to keep them informed. Regular communication with them should be a top priority. Update them on company news and celebrate birthdays and other milestones. Make your communication personal and personable, whether it's a letter, a brochure, a call or an email.

2. Become a valuable resource. The more value you offer, the more a client will depend on you. Don't hesitate to share information they may find useful, whether or not it benefits you in any way. Similarly, don't bombard them with irrelevant news or offers you know won't interest them.

3. Be honest – always. No long-term relationship will survive if the two parties aren't honest with each other. Be open and honest in all of your dealings and communications. Clients are smarter than many people think. They know when they are being sold, misled or manipulated. Even "little white lies" can damage your reputation. Dishonesty destroys integrity, and without it, you'll never cultivate the kind of long-term relationships you and your business need.

4. Meet deadlines. Your word is your bond. Never forget it. When you continually miss deadlines or meetings, you lose integrality and trust. If you commit to doing something, your clients should never doubt that it will happen.

5. Eliminate surprises. No one likes surprises, especially when they are unpleasant. Keep clients informed so they don't miss important news or events, or so they are aware of changes or delays in orders. Even if the news is not positive, knowing is always better than being surprised.

6. Treat clients as people, not income streams. Every client has unique likes, preferences, issues, needs, wants and concerns. The more you understand and identify with clients as people, the stronger your bond will become.

7. Appreciate client loyalty. Never become complacent, especially when you've nurtured a long-term relationship. Express your gratitude and look for ways to say, "Thank you for your business."

8. Make it easy for your clients to buy and keep buying. Lower the barriers to purchasing from you. Shop your own business and think about what could have been easier. Even better, ask your clients how to improve their experience.

Making these ideas part of your everyday approach will let you nurture relationships, drive repeat business and build a long-term client base. These loyal clients will become the foundation for referrals and word-of-mouth marketing, the least expensive and most effective type of marketing any business can use.

*"It's not what you say,
but how you say it."*

It's All About You!

CHAPTER 15

Respect

IN A WORK environment, we hear a lot about the need to respect your coworkers and your boss, but people rarely talk about respecting clients. Why don't we just respect everybody, including family, coworkers, a boss and, oh, clients, too? Clients deserve just as much respect as others you encounter at work or in any setting. When we talk about respecting clients, there are three areas of focus.

1. Respecting them in every interaction.

2. Respecting them when they are not present.

3. Respecting their decisions, no matter what they are, whether in your favor or not.

While it should go without saying, you should show respect to your clients every time you interact with them, whether in person, on the phone, or in writing. It's surprising how often this doesn't happen. For example, I received the following email from someone who was having a hard time accepting the fact that respect may be a thing of the past. She wrote:

> *I called a place of business the other day asking for an employee by their first name. Then, I heard a click. Hmmm. I called back and politely told the receptionist that we must have been disconnected accidentally. The person on the other end said, "It didn't disconnect. I hung up on you." I asked, "Huh? Why did you do that?" She yelled back, "There are 200 employees here and you gave me someone's first name!" There was a long pause. I finally said, "Okay," but before I could finish, there was a click. She had hung up on me again. Help me understand. Is respect a dated concept?"*

No, respect is not outdated, but unfortunately people don't treat clients with respect anymore. This employee simply chose to adopt a negative attitude and behaved disrespectfully. Instead of hanging up, the employee could have asked a wide range of questions to try to find the person being called or to locate someone else who could have helped. The same day, I heard this anecdote.

> *"I went to the FedEx office to get some cards made and laminated. I arrived early and waited outside for about*

five minutes for them to open, so I was the first person at the counter. I was being helped when a man behind me interrupted saying, "I am only here for a pick-up. Can you help me and then finish with her?" I watched quietly to see what would happen. The sales associate calmly said, "I am helping this client right now, but Tom will be back in a few seconds and he will be glad to help you. Or, if I finish first, I will help you."

It's not what you say, but how you say it. This is a perfect example of how one employee showed respect to both clients. First, the employee respected the time of the early arrival by politely refusing to interrupt her service. At the same time, this employee respected the person who wanted to cut in line by responding politely and offering a solution instead of simply saying no.

Common courtesy goes a long way and is so easy to give, yet so often it seems as if our society has lost sight of this simple behavior. Working with an unreasonable client is most challenging and where you are most likely to fail to act with respect. Yet often, an angry client is not upset with <u>you</u>, but with a situation or their experience. You just happen to be in the line of fire. Keep calm, focus on the person, listen actively so that you can clearly understand the problem and try to help. Keeping your cool not only helps the individual calm down, but it will impress other clients who may witness the exchange. In some cases, it may even resolve the issue.

Showing respect when a client is not present is not only the right thing to do, but also demonstrates your integrity and gains the respect of your colleagues. And in most cases, what's said behind someone's back rarely stays there. For example, a first grade teacher was exchanging pleasantries with the mother of one of her students after school as if they were great friends. Later that night, the parent got a call from a friend of hers who had been a substitute teacher at the school the same day. During lunch, the same teacher who had acted so friendly had been ridiculing this mother and joking with other teachers about her lack of parenting skills and her out of control child. Needless to say, there were significant repercussions from this poor judgment and lack of respect. It doesn't matter if a client is present or not. Always be respectful.

Finally, respect means accepting clients' decisions without hesitation. Many salespeople get angry when clients opt to buy from someone else. They wish them ill and hope the product or service they bought won't work so they can say, "I told you so." Others cut the client off, a short-sighted move as there is no telling if the client would have come back in the future.

> *Show respect to your clients every time you interact with them, whether in person, on the phone, or in writing.*

Instead of letting anger take over, treat every client decision—positive or negative—with respect. View them as opportunities to learn so that the next time the client will buy from you. Follow up in a few weeks and have a polite, non-threatening conversation with your client. Find out why you lost the sale. Ask why they made the decision to go somewhere else. Learn what you might have done differently and what you can do in the future. Visit the business that won the client's business and go through the purchasing process. How did it feel? What did you learn that can help you improve?

Respect your clients and their decisions, value their time and treat them as people, not revenue streams. When you invest in your clients, they'll invest in you as well.

"Exceptional service creates the sale."

It's All About You!

CHAPTER 16

Change Your Way of Thinking

THERE ARE PEOPLE who believe that change is not necessary or that things can't change. They accept that the status quo is the only choice. This couldn't be further from the truth. People change every day, physically, intellectually and emotionally. Physically, we all age, our bodies change for better or worse. Intellectual change is a necessity in today's rapidly changing, technology-driven world. Just think about how people communicate today versus even a few years ago. Emotionally, we change because of the experiences we have or choose to have.

Everyone has the ability to change. But, before anyone can change, they must have a desire to change and a willingness to allow change to take place. You can determine the direction for your life, your profession or your business. And your action – or inaction – contributes to what changes occur and how quickly.

Even your attitude can impact your ability to change. If you have an attitude that change is impossible, then you won't change. If you think positively and believe change will take place, most of the time it does. Change, like your attitude, is contagious. If you bring a negative attitude to work, see problems instead of solutions, complain about the job, customers and co-workers, pretty soon others will too. They will begin to see their world and their abilities through your eyes. It's easy to cop a bad attitude. However, if you bring a positive attitude to work, look for solutions, compliment others, help others and focus on teamwork, your environment will reflect that. Others will start to improve because of your positive expectations or encouragement. People will collaborate more and look for solutions instead of whining about problems. Not only will your work environment improve, but your customers will have more pleasant experiences and want to come back to your company and conduct repeat business.

Change is a continual process and it takes time. Change happens when people look at past "choices" with new knowledge and insights, and when they consider future events and decisions with better perspectives and awareness.

For example, have you ever considered that no matter who you are or what you do, everybody is selling somebody something? We all spend more of our time selling than we realize. Virtually every interaction involves sales of some kind, whether you are employed or not. When you call a repairman and he says he'll be there next Tuesday and you say, "Oh don't you have something sooner?" you are selling him on the idea of coming out now. When you let the neighborhood kids play basketball in your driveway, you are selling them on the idea that you are the "cool" parents, when in reality you want to keep an eye on your kids. When you sell the idea, perhaps by offering refreshments, you avoid the argument. As a bonus, your neighbors appreciate the fact that you are keeping an eye on their kids like a good neighbor. When your hairdresser uses "product" in your hair, they are selling you on the idea of using it at home. When teachers reward students for returning homework on time, they are selling them on completing their work.

It's estimated that people spend 40 percent of their time in non-sales selling, either at work or at home. We persuade, influence and convince to act, think, believe or choose, all without purchasing anything. Everyone is selling something.

Additionally, one out of every nine workers in the United States earns a living by selling, by trying to get others to make a purchase. They sell stocks, cars, T-shirts, art, machines, food, tickets and thousands of other items. They work in fancy offices, in simple stores, in call centers, in booths on a street or from the comfort of their own homes. With technology salespeople can showcase their products and services anywhere and at anytime, create a customized experience and enable personal interaction.

Everyone is a salesperson. But, what are successful sales people selling? Let's look at all the "salespeople" in a grocery store.

- Store managers who provide carts for children so they can enjoy shopping with their parents are selling parents on their store (a more pleasant shopping experience, an educational opportunity for your children). They also sell more products because parents often purchase at least one item that their kids put in their carts (that's why you don't want to bring your kids to the market).

- Baggers are usually the last person you talk to in the market. In most stores, baggers stand quietly and pack your goods. Yet even with this seemingly mundane job is a sales function. By asking questions about the kind of bag (your own, single, double, paper or plastic) you want, whether or not you want your groceries separated and whether you need help to the car, the bagger is selling you on their ability to efficiently and carefully pack your groceries. They give customers confidence that their food will make it home safely. What better reason to come back?

- Produce managers who polish and stock while you shop are selling you on the idea that you will always get fresh food.

- The "samples" staff members sell multiple products at once by creating and serving recipes and by having the ingredients conveniently on hand for purchase.

- The meat department and deli counter staff always ask two questions: "Would you like to taste?" and "Can I get you something else?" They are selling your food that you might not have tried and that you now know you enjoy.

- Even food manufacturers are selling customers in the stores. They purchase premium end caps to create a need or want as customers walk by. If you are a brand loyalist, you will automatically buy more when you see the end cap. If you are new to the brand, you are more apt to stop and consider trying it. Every package is designed to catch your eye and sell you on the product. The entire store is arranged in a way so that you will see and try new items. The best selling items are usually on the top and bottom shelves, not at eye level. Prices are small so they are the last thing seen. Every piece of merchandise is designed to make you think, "I want that," without ever thinking about price. Why else would honey be sold in a bear-shaped jar?

What's important to notice is that these individuals are not selling price or products. They are selling value. There is value to the parents shopping with kids; value in knowing your groceries are fresh and safely packed; value in being able to quickly and easily create a new, tasty meal and value in being able to try new foods before you buy them.

Look at what they just did—they were selling, even to your kids! Who knew?

Salespeople who create an exceptional experience for their customer know that a sale will follow. Extraordinary salespeople don't actually sell, they help customers buy. They are intent on helping customers find the right product or service for their own situation. They know the customer always comes first. At Amazon, founder and CEO Jeff Bezos always makes sure that there is one empty chair in every meeting to remind others that the most important person in the room is the customer.

Recognizing this, salespeople must develop an ability to actively listen and quickly find the fine line between what customers need and what they want. They must strike the right balance between the two in order to delight the customer. A single person with a dog who is house hunting most likely isn't interested in a five bedroom home or a two bedroom condo. While they need a place to live, they want a place with enough room to live comfortably and play outside, like a two bedroom home with a yard. They need to find a home that works for their dog first.

Building long-term customer relationships is extremely important. It comes down to having a consistent process that is adhered to at every step of a customer interaction by every person. Salespeople learn to listen, evaluate variables, identify key drivers, overcome objections and find ways to reach agreement—without burning bridges. Salespeople learn to ask for what they want. Closing a sale is part art and part science. Great salespeople know how to close relationships. They are persistent and inventive, and look for solutions for overcoming obstacles and objections.

Professionally or as part of daily life everyone is selling. As salespeople or not, the skills we learn and use will be invaluable for the rest of your business – and personal – life.

Who knew? You are a salesperson.

It is time to change your way of thinking. First, however, it's important to decide what you want to change. Then, identify steps you can take to start on the path to change and finally, follow through, consistently. If you stumble, and you will, get back up and keep going. Check your attitude. Identify the things you can influence and control. There are always things you can control and things you have no control over. Even so, everyone has a choice in every circumstance. Instead of complaining or feeling angry or frustrated about a situation or event, think about how things can be changed to drive a different outcome. Then take steps to make it happen. Be careful not to overlook yourself and focus only on things and others around you.

> *Salespeople who create an exceptional experience for their customer, know that the sale will follow.*

Think about where you want to go professionally. Put a plan in place and work it. Include small, simple actions like changing how you dress or identifying people you wish to emulate and then studying them and learning from their success. Small changes can have huge impacts, like never using "I" to start a sentence in an email or letter. As Lowes Hotel chairman Jonathan M. Tisch says, "My boss told me that whenever you're writing a letter—and now it applies to emails today—never start a paragraph with the word 'I,' because that immediately sends a message that you are more important than the person that you're communicating with."

I am sure that the first thing you plan to do differently is to change. Are you ready?

It's All About You!

CHAPTER 17

Feedback – The Silver Bullet?

MOST OF THE time salespeople interact with customers, colleagues and others believing that they are working in the best way possible. They believe that they are doing the right thing. This belief is not a bad thing, in fact it's important because without confidence and belief in their abilities, salespeople would not succeed. From time to time, however, it's important to solicit feedback to identify weaknesses and find better ways to work. This may seem obvious. Yet most people never proactively seek feedback, or at least feedback that really matters. Even when provided, sales professionals in general are paying less and less attention to feedback. Increasingly they believe that negative feedback only comes from people with an axe to grind. And, while they embrace positive feedback, they don't use it to improve their skills.

Candid, constructive, positive and negative feedback is one of the most important tools at a salesperson's disposal. Even salespeople who do everything right and succeed in achieving their goals, always can find opportunities to improve. Feedback helps salespeople learn, grow and strengthen their skills. For salespeople who regularly stop the sale, the worst thing – and the easiest thing – to do is to explain it away, avoid and ignore feedback from anyone.

It's easy to explain away a lost sale without taking any responsibility: the customers didn't really want to buy, they were loyal to another brand they didn't have the money or financing. The harder thing to do is to find the problem and correct it, to proactively seek out feedback, listen to it with an open mind and make changes. Even the smallest changes can make a big difference.

Gathering, analyzing and using feedback is not a new concept. Marketing teams use it every day. Have you ever seen a commercial, noticed it went away and then realized the same commercial came back weeks or months later? Consumer feedback informs advertisers that this particular spot is achieving their goals. So, they run it again for as long as it remains effective. The same is true for commercials that run back to back, especially ones with powerful catch phrases or slogans. Feedback shows that repeating something over and over makes it sticks, often for years. For example, consider

"Where's the Beef?" (Wendy's) and "Got Milk?" (The Milk Advisory Board). Finally, companies use focus groups, people who represent their target audiences, to secure feedback on existing or new products or services. They use this feedback to make the products better and to ensure the products or services are something their customers will buy.

Just as in these examples, feedback can help salespeople understand where they are effective and help them learn how they can become even better.

Most people are afraid to admit that they may have contributed to a lost sale. No one likes to feel like they failed. Others are afraid that seeking help or feedback will be seen as weakness by management and put their jobs in jeopardy. Yet overcoming that fear is the best approach to success.

Feedback can come from many places. Start with yourself. Honestly critique the experience. Ask yourself, "What did I do right? What could I have done better?" "What shouldn't I have done?" "How do I know?" "How should I improve?"

Think about your customers' reactions and responses during the time you spent with them.

- Did you ask questions that helped you learn about the customer and how they will use the product or service?
- Were the customers engaged?
- Did you get the answers you needed to help you show them the right solution?
- Did you listen to their answers?

- How clearly did you understand their needs, wants and desires?
- Did you give them the best possible service and reasons to buy from you?
- How did the time you spent with your customers feel? What did your gut tell you?
- Was the conversation forced or comfortable?
- Did you feel like the customers were eager to leave?
- Did it feel like the customers wanted to learn more?
- Did you confuse the customers?
- Did you make a connection with the customers?
- Did you communicate with them, on the same level?
- Overall, did they enjoy the experience?
- Did you learn from that experience?

If your answers to any of these were less than desirable, think about what you could do differently. Be honest. There is always room for improvement. Even the best salesperson can improve.

Next, ask your colleagues, especially if you aren't sure about how to improve. Ask them what they would have done in the same situation, listen and learn from their experience. Ask what they observed and what specific advice they'd have for that situation. Remember, it's not the customer who was bad, it's what happened during the process, it's what you did, that was bad. If they say nothing, ask someone else and keep asking until you learn something.

Finally, ask your customers, the ones who purchased one time, the loyal ones who give you repeat business and those you lost. Find out what they liked about working with you, what frustrated them and/or why they opted not to buy or not to come back. Listen with an open mind, take notes and consider their input as constructive criticism. Then, look for ways to change your approach, your behavior, so you can improve.

Feedback is important when performance is strong as well. If your customer appointments are up, sales performance and volume is increasing and repeat business is booming, find out why. What are you doing now that you may not have been doing in the past? Identify the differences and focus on making them part of your ongoing approach.

Asking for feedback is not always easy. These six questions will help you secure clear, actionable input, starting with the most important.

1. If they didn't buy from you, ask customers,"Why not?" Use this to help you identify what went wrong and what you could have done to change the situation.

2. If they did buy, ask them, "What we could do to improve the business?"

3. Ask what they think could be better about the product or service.

4. Ask what you could have done to make the process or experience better.

5. Be sure you understand the feedback. Paraphrase major points and ask clarifying questions.

6. Be appreciative. Thank people for their feedback. Remember that getting feedback is like receiving a gift. People have to care enough to give it.

Learning about performance from different sources (including yourself), will help you correct your deficiencies and capitalize on your strengths.

Regardless of why you sought out feedback, once you receive it, you have to make a choice. You can choose to learn from it and use it to your benefit to improve, or you can ignore it and stick with the status quo. Who knew? It's completely up to you.

Hopefully, most professionals will choose to use it to their advantage. Using feedback is a different skill than accepting feedback. And, it's a skill that requires practice.

Develop the plan to improve. Good feedback helps you identify what actions will lead to improvement. Assess the behaviors or actions that have been identified that could need improvement. This is why getting specific feedback is important. If you have been told that you don't truly listen to customers, ask for specific examples of when this happened and how you can change your behavior. You could have been told that you don't let people finish their thoughts, you jump to conclusions, you don't give people your full attention or you don't maintain eye contact. Based on this type of specific feedback, put a plan in place to improve.

Ask for coaching. Having a coach can help keep you accountable. Work with someone you trust who can watch you in action and give suggestions about small adjustments that can make a big difference.

Practice. Once you determine how you want to change or what new skills you want to develop, it is important to consciously practice them. If you are trying to improve your listening skills, you may need to be aware of and control your tendency to prematurely respond. As you practice, ask for feedback. At the end of a conversation, ask your customers if they felt that you listened to and heard their needs. Ask how you could have done better.

Look for and evaluate the results. When you use these new skills or if you change your behaviors, be sure to evaluate whether or not the changes are having an impact. While your intentions may be good, your new approach may not bring the results you are seeking. There may be other actions you can take that are more effective.

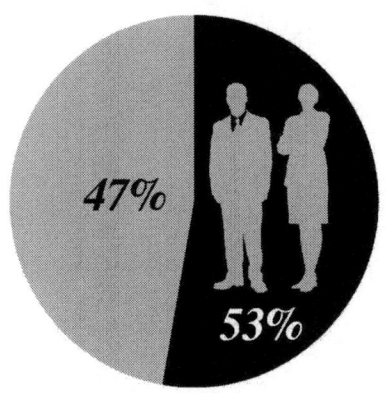

47%

53%

53% *of customers altered their buying habits for one or more years after having a bad experience*

Remember, not all feedback has to do with improvement or making changes. Positive feedback can help you understand what works and what you should continue to do.

It's clear that feedback is an essential tool for any business professional. Just as you rely on others to provide the advice you need to succeed, you should be willing to provide feedback to your colleagues. Make a point to give one or two people some positive feedback each day—without any negative feedback attached to it. All too often people don't hear about the positive things they do, only the negative. If your feedback is sought, use the steps you've learned in this chapter to provide constructive, specific and actionable input that can make a positive difference for a colleague.

It's rare that you will find a bad customer. More often it's the salesperson or what they did during the sales process. Getting a customer to like you is half the battle. If you talk to the customer and engage them at their level, you'll succeed. Remember, people don't care about how much you know, they care about how much you care.

So, what can you do to improve? In looking for an answer to this, everyone looks for the proverbial silver bullet or magic formula. Seeking out and using feedback may be as close as anyone will ever get to finding one of these. Asking for and acting on feedback is a simple process, and it doesn't cost a penny.

It would be a shame not to take advantage of it. After all, there is always room for improvement.

Who knew?

It's All About You!

About the Author

RICHARD F. LIBIN, president of APB, is focused on ensuring that the management and staff of APB's clients keep pace with today's sophisticated and more demanding customers, while excelling in customer satisfaction and maximizing gross profit in every department.

Mr. Libin has taken a leadership position in adapting new technologies for improved sales and service performance since he joined APB in 1980 as a management consultant. Since then he has worked closely with businesses using a hands-on, on-site approach to develop management and sales teams, which are more successful in achieving predetermined objectives.

Prior to joining APB, Mr. Libin was affiliated with one of the largest New England auto auctions, a Chevrolet dealership in the Boston area. During this time he developed a keen understanding for every facet of the business, starting as a technician and working his way to service advisor, assistant service manager, sales professional and ultimately, sales manager. In addition, Mr. Libin managed an independent towing, repair and body business, working closely with customers and professional teams. His experience with both wholesale and retail customers gave him a solid foundation and understanding of the internal chemistry of both service and sales departments.

Mr. Libin writes recurring articles for *WARDSAUTO'S IdeaXchange, The American Salesman, EyesonSales* and *Sales Gravy*. His first book, "Who Stopped the Sale?" was originally published in 2010.